ACKNOWLEDGMENTS

There are four groups of individuals I need to thank for this book project. First, to my family, Melanie, Isaiah, Sutherland, and Cailan, for their support and encouragement—I love you! Second, without the help of Christine Scheller, Romy and Neil Godding, Cristin Novak, Lance Emma, and Dr. Peter Riola, this book would have never made it off the ground. Thank you for all your hard work! Third, to the staff at Calvary Chapel Schools, for their service to the Lord—I really appreciate you! Fourth, to Pastors Chuck Smith and Brian Brodersen, for allowing me to serve the Lord in a wonderful Christian school environment.

PREFACE

I have some vivid memories of my educational upbringing—some good, some bad. Yet, all were learning experiences. First, there was Mrs. Harrigher, my third grade teacher. She was amazing. I remember her reading books to our class on warm New Mexico days. The fan blowing and our minds expanding created a memorable, wonderful, and comforting experience. Mrs. Harrigher sent me postcards from around the world (she traveled a lot) and helped me develop a love for learning. I was struck by her care and loved her class.

Then there was my fourth grade teacher, whom I will not mention by name, who provided me with an example of the opposite teaching style of my beloved Mrs. Harrigher. I learned, I'm sure, some material; but more than anything, I learned what the principal's office looked like and what his voice sounded like when he was upset. I also learned what a book looks like when a teacher uses it as a weapon on my friend Andy's head.

Then there were my upper grade years. Mr. Chamberlain, Mr. Petriliak, and others helped shape my life and give direction to a youth more interested in music than in class work. Nonetheless, I made it through, and my school years left an impression on me.

If there is one thing I learned throughout my formative educational years, it is that education is a powerful tool; a tool that can build up, or a tool that can break down; a system that can be used for good purposes or wrong purposes; learning can be a time of growth or a time of stunting growth. The bottom line is that education has a lasting influence on students. This is why the teaching and learning process is crucial: education has a lasting influence on the lives of children and adults. And more importantly, for the Christian, education can have an eternal purpose. The reason for this work on the philosophy of education is straightforward. My aim is to discuss and develop a purely Christocentric view of education. Put a little more simply, I want to converse about how Jesus learned, taught, and how He demonstrated and modeled for us a truly "divine" plan of education.

The overview of this work is summarized by three words: foundation, framework, and fruit. First is the foundation. Here, I develop a Christ-based philosophy of education utilizing the words of Jesus. Second is the framework. Once again, using the words of Jesus, I construct a paradigm or matrix upon which one can base educational outcomes; it is essentially a model of educational direction. I also briefly talk about what the rest of the New Testament has to say regarding this framework. Finally, I discuss the fruit of the educational endeavor. Though I do not offer concrete ideas for curriculum and books, I do offer some basic principles by which one can abide when choosing curriculum. Throughout the work, I have attempted to balance the cognitive with the practical. I give a brief history of the various educational philosophies, both secular and sacred, as well as a general historical overview of some of the key players in Christian education.

Though at times I get a little "heady," my intention is not to show off any philosophical skill (of which I have little), but rather to lay a foundation that is needed for the construction of a Christ-based philosophy of education. However, I have overtly attempted to give concrete suggestions and principles educators can use (at least as principles) to explain why a Christ-based education is important.

Before I begin, however, I must state my bias. Every living human being carries some kind of bias, or angle of approach. My bias is rooted in the historical, evangelistic Christian faith. I do not pretend to be anything else. So, my bias is going to reflect my worldview. The following paragraphs will help clarify my position on the

Christian faith, and will hopefully give the reader a sense of "where I am coming from."

Approach

Paul of Tarsus, in the age in which he lived, was emphatic about several key aspects concerning the new Christian faith: one, it is centered on the person of Christ: His life, death, and resurrection; two, Christ has preeminence in all things; and three, God has "spoken" in the person of Jesus Christ. For Paul, Christianity was about Jesus Christ—crucified and declared. Paul unapologetically defended the veracity and objective reality of the Christian faith.

In the course of this discussion, I will declare that what was true in Paul's age concerning the life and faith of Christianity is also true today in relation to how Christianity is to be lived out; and specifically, how a Christ-based philosophy of education is paramount for implications related to truth as played out in the arena of knowledge and education. Stated another way, the person of Christ must not only inform the "religious" nature of man, but the praxis of man.

Just as Paul stressed the centrality of Jesus Christ, I, too, will stress the person of Christ—His words, teachings, and methodologies—as the basis for educational paradigms, foundations, and frameworks.

Before the area of education is tackled, we must first take a look at foundational issues concerning biblical Christianity. As an orthodox (Bible-believing) Christian, I subscribe to the historic Christian creeds and the inerrant trustworthiness of Scripture. Furthermore, to help clarify my position for the sake of this discussion, I will state three propositions summarizing the direction of my approach and then briefly comment on each proposition.

First, I believe that God has spoken clearly in both the person of Christ and in His Word, the Bible. Second, the Christian faith is not only a matter of belief, of feeling, or even of action, but it encompasses objective truth. Third, because Christianity is true and defensible, it is worthy to be practiced and lived out.

God Has Spoken

The fact that God has spoken in the person of Christ is the one of the essential components of the Christian faith. Hebrews chapter one clearly states that "God, who at sundry times and in divers manners spake in time past unto the fathers by the prophets, hath in these last days spoken unto us by his Son, whom he hath appointed heir of all things ..." (Heb 1:1–2 KJV). So, how has God spoken? First, it is in the person of Christ (the "revelation"). Second, it is through Scripture, the revealing of His will. Essentially, God's will is found in Christ and declared through His Word—the Bible.

The Christian worldview is, at its root, the declaration that Christ is who the Bible says He is—Lord and Savior, and therefore, the *Logos* and truth of God. In addition, if Christ is truth (as He, in the Bible, states in Jn 14:6), then Jesus must be the fulfillment of objective reality.

If the Christian faith is to be the fortress amidst disbelief and opposing religions, it must clearly set forth the declaration that Christ and His Word are truth and that God has spoken through them. The person of Christ must be proclaimed, taught, and studied. For, logically speaking, if Christ were not who He said He was, then Christian education, and ultimately, Christianity, is meaningless. Therefore, the basis of the Christian faith states that since God spoke to humanity in the person of Christ, as is clearly taught in the Word, Christians will adhere to, believe in, and teach doctrine as found in the Bible.

Christianity Is Truth

In our present society, relativism is the reigning philosophy. It presents all truth as subjective, or relative. People often say, "Do whatever feels good"; "your truth is yours, mine is mine"; and, "all roads lead to heaven." Philosophies such as these demonstrate the mentality that there is not "one truth" or "one way" by which to verify something; they illustrate, as already stated, the subjective. Subjectivism is the belief that one cannot know anything for sure because of others' differing experiences and viewpoints. Subjectivism is the motto of the modern world.

In stark contrast to subjectivism is objective truth. Objective truth defends reason and empirical fact. It provides an intellectual foundation for verifiable standards of truth and value. According to Jesus, He is objective truth, and therefore, for the Christian, the truth He is and teaches must be defended. Jesus, Himself, as stated previously, said, "I am the way, the truth, and the life" (Jn 14:6). Jesus left little room for doubt concerning truth—He is it! I appreciate what Harry Blamires states, "You cannot construct truth at all: you can only discover it" (Blamires 112 CM). Further, he writes, "You cannot make truth. You reside in the truth" (Blamires 113 CM). As Christians, we reside in the truth of God in Christ, nothing more, nothing less.

The second area of revealed truth is the Bible. Internal evidence suggests that the Bible is called "the very words of God," utilizing titles such as "God's testimony," and "Thus saith the Lord." And if it is God's Word, it therefore must be true, objectively so. Noted Christian scholar Dr. John W. Montgomery carefully stresses the need to return to an objective view of the Christian faith. Montgomery states, "Christianity is unique in claiming intrinsic, not merely extrinsic, connection with empirical reality which is the subject of scientific investigation" (Montgomery 277 ST). Therefore, Scripture "is inspired as the theological norm—as God's authoritative message in matters spiritual ... historical ... and scientific" (Montgomery 315 ST). Hence, all of reality is subject to God's revealed truth—the Bible.

The Bible and Christ as objective truth by no means declare that every "issue" related to reality is taught or covered in the Bible or in Christ's teachings. Fields such as science have ample room for discovery and investigation. What is being said is that the Bible is the framework upon which the world should be viewed. In essence, it declares the "outline" of existence: creation, the fall, history, redemption, and the consummation of all things. It does not pretend to give the "specifics" of every topic to every field. The Bible, if you will, is the blueprint for understanding reality.

Though it is not my intention to give a theological or apologetic treatise on the objective reality of the Bible, it is important to recognize its veracity as a facet for practical application. As a Christian, I must ask myself, "What role should the Bible play in life (and from an educational standpoint—curriculum and school)?" The answer—and I think that most orthodox biblical scholars would agree—is that it should play a very central role. Truth as found in the Bible should be considered in all subject matters and studied for all areas of investigation. Because "Christian faith is not blind faith or credulity; it is grounded in fact" (Montgomery 79 FF), the truth of the Christian claim should manifest itself in all academic, civic, and personal realms. The Bible as the objective truth of God is trustworthy in all fields of inquiry.

Christianity Should Be Lived Out

Because God has spoken in the person of Christ and His Word, and is therefore an objective reality, it logically follows that the truth of Christianity must be "lived out," as the verification of our faith. In order to call myself a Christian, I need to live as a Christian. In order for the claims of Christ to have a living reality within my life, I need to live the realities of Christ in my walk. Areas such as biblical authority, politics and religion, love and law, the devotional life, evangelism and renewal, education, and art are all extremely important areas to live out according to the Christian worldview. In all these areas, stress is placed upon the "living" aspect of the Christian life, which gives rise to the question, how does a Christian approach the realm and ideas of everyday living?

Essentially, for the Christian, God must be the center of all human endeavors. In addition, what is true in the social realm is true in the personal realm; in Christ, we find the answer. Therefore, we can confidently enjoy, love, and devote ourselves to the tasks He has laid before us. Our devotion and love of the Lord are intricate parts of our faith. Worship, praise, thanksgiving, and so forth, are as important as orthodox theology and biblical truth; the two elements go hand in hand.

As a Christian, I must yearn for a strong biblical faith as well as a life of devotion and love towards the Lord; a Christian life is about the head and heart, the mind and soul. It is the privilege for all Christians to, as the our Lord states, "Love the Lord thy God with all thy heart, and with all thy soul, and with all thy mind" (Mt 22:37 KJV).

As part of the "living out" element of Christianity, this discourse will specifically deal with how Christianity is to be practiced in the educational realm. It will examine, with the person of Christ as the foundation (declaration, student, and teacher) for education, and seek to develop a framework upon which Christ's words act as the springboard for educational integration—drawing a parallel between how Christ learned as a student and how He taught as an adult.

INTRODUCTION: HISTORY AND PHILOSOPHIES

Before a Christ-based philosophy of education is discussed, attention must be given to the prevailing philosophies of education that do exist, both secular and Christian. What I do not want to naively suggest is that the other Christian philosophies of religious education are not biblical, or that they do not adhere to a biblical standard or worldview. In many circumstances, this is not the case. Many of the methodologies do attempt to construct a philosophy of education that is both biblically astute and theologically pertinent. However, for many of these philosophies, a philosophical matrix or framework is first established, and then attempts are made to reconcile it with the Bible. I see this as largely backward. The approach I take in this discussion is to let the words, actions, and methods of Jesus Christ speak for themselves. Rather than taking an outside-to-inside approach, I begin from the inside (the Bible and specifically Jesus' words) and let it affect the outside (the philosophy and framework). I yearn to let Jesus speak for Himself and let a Christ-based philosophy of education organically rise from who He is and how and what He teaches.

But first, a brief history of education in the church is in store.

Jesus and the Apostles

Jesus was obviously concerned with education, for in His closing earthy statement, He commands His disciples to "go therefore and a make disciples of all nations, *teaching* ..." The disciples were educators, though not in the formal sense. Their mission was to teach the world of Christ. It is safe to conclude that Jesus and the disciples were the beginning of the Christian education movement. From the ministry first established by the early disciples, six major areas of history are seen: the early church fathers, the golden age of church fathers, the Middle Age leaders, the Reformers, the modern church leaders, and the Postmodern Era.

The Early Church Fathers

The early church fathers were those individuals who lived roughly from AD 100–300. Christians in this era were concerned with several key elements: surviving (due to persecution), defending the faith (apologetics), and providing a clear Christian worldview. Men such as Justin Martyr (ca. 100–165), Tatian (ca. 110–180), Theophilus of Antioch (ca. 180–190), and Tertullian (ca. 160–250 AD) were influential in defending Christianity from heresy and, in turn, explaining Christianity to the masses. During this era, two major "schools" of study arose: Alexandrian and Carthaginian. Clement of Alexandria (155–215) and Origen (185–254) led the Alexandrian school. This school sought to balance Greek philosophy, methodology, and biblical truth. From the school arose strong allegorical modes of biblical interpretation. The second school, Carthaginian, was more interested in polity, government, and sound "orthodox" doctrine; it was led by Tertullian and Cyprian (ca. 200–258). Additionally, the catechumenate school system was used to teach the Christian faith to new believers, which, in turn, allowed for catechetical schools to arise. In any case, the early church had a definite emphasis on teaching and learning.

The Golden Age of Church Fathers

The golden age of church fathers took place during the approximate years of AD 200–500. The men in this era were concerned with three pertinent issues: the development of the Canon and creeds, the relation between church and state, and the proclamation of the faith through missions, schools, and the organized church. Leaders during this era included Athanasius (ca. 296–350), Eusebius (ca. 260–341), Jerome (ca. 331), Ambrose (ca. 339), John Chrysostom (ca. 347), and Augustine of Hippo (ca. 354). Not only were these men influential in determining the creeds of the church, writing its history, and promoting its missions, but they also discussed the role it played in relation to the state and the world (missions), and translated the Bible (Jerome) into Latin. John Chrysostom was one of the first individuals to write a book specifically dealing with the education of Christian children, *Concerning the Education of Children.*

As with the prior era, schools were set up to promote Christian ideals and promote the gospel. The Syrian school tended to be of the historical/grammatical (literalist interpretation) methodology, while the Alexandrian school maintained its focus on the allegorical interpretation.

The Middle Age Leaders

The Middle Ages occurred roughly between AD 500–1400. The emphasis during this era was the domination of the Roman Church, religious and political strife (rise of Islam and European states leading to crusades), the split between the Eastern church (Orthodox) and the Western church (Roman), and the rise of monasticism, mysticism, and scholasticism.

Educationally, scholasticism is of crucial importance. Here, the church utilized the frameworks of the Trivium and Quadrivium (Liberal Arts) as a means of educating its people. Scholasticism was the attempt by men of the era to pursue a reasonable faith; it sought to organize theology with logic and reason. Three "schools" of thought arose from this time: Realism ("I believe that I may know"); Moderate Realism ("particular things are most real to us, but universals are most real in themselves"); and Nominalism ("dogma is not rationally demonstrable, but must be accepted on the authority of the Bible").

Not only did modern universities arise from the Middle Ages, but men such as Bede (672–735), Anselm (ca. 1033: Realist), Thomas Aquinas (ca. 1225: Moderate Realist), and William of Ockham (1280: Nominalist) influenced the thought, philosophy, and education of the era. Other leaders such as Alcuin (735–804, who may have reintroduced the Trivium and Catechism in Europe)—Hrabanus Maurus (776–856), Peter Abelard (1079–1142), and John Gerson (1363–1429) helped educate both in the religious realm and in the secular realm, where they tutored both clergy and royalty.

Reformers

With the onset of the Reformation, the modern church began to arise. The modern era of church history is characterized by several important facets: reform and separation of the "established church"; rise in learning and education due to the printing press and Protestant ideals; growing influence of the Protestant Church and biblical literacy; and evangelism and "world growth" due to exploration and colonization.

Influential men in this era were pre-Reformers: John Huss (1369–1415) and John Wycliffe (1324–1384); and later Reformers Martin Luther (1483–1546), Erasmus of Rotterdam (1466–1536), John Calvin (1509–1564), and William Tyndale (1494–1536).

It is safe to say that the "modern" educational movement began with the Reformers. Because stress was placed upon reading and understanding Scripture, education for the "common man" arose, and thereby influenced nations and ultimately the world. Many of the leading Reformers were either highly educated men, who went on to form schools, or men who had taught at universities and applied their knowledge to the cause of Christ.

The Modern Church Era

The modern church can roughly be said to have taken place between the years 1520 and 1920. This was an era of reform, revivalism, rationalism, and missions. As previously mentioned, the Reformation had a great impact, not only in the newly developed

Protestant churches, but in the Roman churches as well. As the Protestant ideals took greater shape, they were transported throughout the Western World via exploration, missions, and evangelism. The Roman Church, likewise, had its own reformation and took its principles to the farthest parts of the globe. However, the Modern Era had problems as well: revolution, wars, materialistic worldviews, and church infighting were all part of the development of the age.

Men such as John Wesley (1703–1791) and George Whitfield (1714–1770) established an evangelical root in both Britain and America. Count Zinzendorf (1700–1760) used evangelism, schools, and music to proclaim the gospel. In America, men such as Jonathan Edwards (1703–1758), and later, D. L. Moody (1837–1899) used mass evangelism to spread the gospel throughout the nation. In England, William Wilberforce (1759–1833) and Charles Spurgeon (1834–1892) spoke to thousands about the Christian message and stressed Christian scholarship and biblical literacy.

Many prominent schools arose during this age as well: Harvard in 1636, William and Mary in 1693, and Princeton in 1754. Most were established as Christian schools of higher learning stressing a worldview compatible with the Bible. Likewise, Robert Raikes (1735–1811) established the Sunday school movement to help educate and assist poor children in England. The Modern Church Era is best seen in light of Christianity's dominance in thought and culture; in essence, many of the Western World's societies became "Christian" in the wide sense of the word.

The Postmodern Era

Whereas the Modern Era is characterized by the Christian worldview, the Postmodern Era can be summarized as a moving away from a Christian worldview, towards a relativistic idea of truth and culture. In a sense, the Postmodern Era is a demise of reason and the exultation of a subjective (relativistic) view of reality.

However, in the orthodox Christian educational realm, truth

stood firm and educational methodologies expanded greatly during the Postmodern Era. Individuals during the Postmodern Era are classified by the school of thought in which they reside.

The Classical/Liberal model (the idea that theological construct is open to change and scientific investigation) was led by men and women such as George Coe (1862–1951), Sophia Fahs (1876–1978), William Bower (1878–1954), Adelaide Case (1887–1948), George Betts (1868–1934), and Ernest Chave (1886–1961).

The Theological or Mainline model sought to establish theological truth about God and man's need for God, and then to educate people accordingly. Leading men and women of this era include: Randolph Miller, Lewis Sherrill (1892–1957), Sara Little, James Smart (1906–1882), Iris Cully, D. Campbell Wyckoff, Howard Grimes, John Westerhoff, Gordon Chamberlin, Rachel Henderlite (1905–1991), Gabriel Moran, and Maria Harris.

The Evangelical/Kerygmatic model was rooted in evangelical modes of interpretation and outreach—stressing biblical authority, "living out" one's faith, and the transmission of "truth" as informed by Scripture. Leaders in this group include: Frank Gaebelein (1907–1983), Lois LeBar, Clarence Benson (1879–1954), Charles Eavey (1889–1974), Harold Mason (1888–1964), Herbert Byrne, Kenneth Gangel, Roy Zuck, James Murch (1892–1972), Lawrence Richards, Donald Joy, Findley B. Edge, and Robert Pazmiño.

The Modern Classical Christian method is a hybrid between the evangelical faith and the medieval methodology of the Trivium and Quadrivium. Leaders in this area are Dorothy Sayers (1893–1957), C. S. Lewis (1898–1963), David Hicks, and Douglas Wilson.

The Postmodern Era, as one can ascertain from the variety of individuals, is a smorgasbord of ideas, methods, and philosophies. Some of the philosophies have direct biblical overtones; others are more related to the latest sociological fads or cultural interests. However, one point remains steadfast in the Postmodern Era—Christian education has increased in size and influence.

The Philosophies: Secular

In the secular realm, five major philosophies of education exist: Perennialism, Progressivism, Essentialism, Existentialism, and Behaviorism. What needs to be stated clearly is that the secular philosophies are by no means purely biblical, and many are what I would classify as anti-Christian. Though some have integrated Christian principles, none of the philosophies, in and of themselves, claim to be a Christian representation of education. These philosophies are rooted in a humanistic order of society rather than in biblical norms. So, why state them? The reason is that religious institutions have utilized various aspects of these philosophies and continue to do so. To adequately address these principles, we need at least a general understanding of them. Each philosophy has many supporters in education circles, both in secular and religious realms. There have been other designations for these secular educational philosophies: idealism, realism, experimentalism, for example; but, for the sake of clarity, I will use the more common terms as mentioned above. Overall, these five schools of thought do not exhaust the list of possible educational philosophies found in the secular world, but they present strong philosophical frameworks used throughout educational groups.

Perennialism

This view is based on fundamental fixed truths. It states that people find truth through reasoning and revelation and that goodness is found in rational thinking. Students are taught to reason through structured lessons and drills, with emphasis placed on the great books of Western culture. Past proponents of Perennialism are Mortimer Adler, Robert Hutchins, and Peter Wolff.

Progressivism

According to Larry J. Shaw, "Progressivism's respect for individuality, its high regard for science, and its receptivity to change harmonized well with the American environment in which it was created. The person most responsible for the success of progressivism was John Dewey (1859–1952). ... Dewey taught that people are social animals who learn well through active interplay with others and that our learning increases when we are engaged in activities that have meaning for us. Book learning, to Dewey, was no substitute for actually doing things. Fundamental to Dewey's epistemology is the notion that knowledge is acquired and expanded as we apply our previous experiences to solving new, meaningful problems" (Shaw http://edweb.sdsu.edu/LShaw/f95syll/philos/phprogr.html).

Dewey, more than any other American, has helped shape and mold American education (especially public education) away from the Judeo-Christian ideals towards a relativistic understanding of the world.

Essentialism

Again, quoting Shaw, "Essentialism refers to the traditional or Back to the Basics approach to education. It is so named because it strives to instill students with the essentials of academic knowledge and character development. The term essentialism as an educational philosophy was originally popularized in the 1930s by the American educator William Bagley (1874–1946) ... essentialism is grounded in a conservative philosophy that accepts the social, political, and economic structure of American society. It contends that schools should not try to reshape society. Rather, essentialists argue, American schools should transmit the traditional moral values and intellectual knowledge that students need to become model citizens. Essentialists believe that teachers should instill such traditional American virtues as respect for authority, perseverance, fidelity to duty, consideration for others, and practicality" (Shaw http://edweb.sdsu.edu/LShaw/f95syll/philos/phessent.html).

Existentialism

Existentialism has a long history of thought, starting with the Christian Soren Kierkegaard (1813–1855). However, throughout the years, it has taken on nihilistic and relativistic overtones. According to Jean Paul Sartre, a proponent of modern existentialism, "Man is nothing else but what he makes of himself. Such is the first principle of existentialism" (Shaw http://edweb.sdsu.edu/LShaw/f95syll/philos/phexist.html).

Shaw comments,

> ... existentialism sprang from a strong rejection of the traditional, essentialist approach to education. Existentialism rejects the existence of any source of objective, authoritative truth about metaphysics, epistemology, and ethics. Instead, individuals are responsible for determining for themselves what is "true" or "false," "right" or "wrong," "beautiful" or "ugly." For the existentialist, there exists no universal form of human nature; each of us has the free will to develop as we see fit" (Shaw http://edweb.sdsu.edu/LShaw/f95syll/philos/phexist.html).

Existentialism believes in the personal interpretation of the world. It is based on the view that the individual defines reality, truth, and goodness. As a result, schools exist to aid children in knowing themselves and their place in society. Students learn what they want and discuss subjects freely.

Behaviorism

"... behaviorism is derived from the belief that free will is an illusion. According to a pure behaviorist, human beings are shaped entirely by their external environment. Alter a person's environment, and you will alter his or her thoughts, feelings, and behavior. Provide positive reinforcement whenever students perform a desired behavior, and soon they will learn to perform the behavior on their own. Behaviorism has its roots in the early 1900s in the work of the Russian experimental psychologist Ivan Pavlov (1848–1936)" (Shaw http://edweb.sdsu.edu/LShaw/f95syll/philos/phbehav.html). J'Anne Ellsworth adds that Behaviorists' focal points are as follows:

- No such thing as free will

- Learning is a physiological response to stimuli
- Human nature is innately neither good nor bad, but is shaped by environment
- Behavior modification
- Contingency management
- Advocates use of positive rather than negative reinforcement to shape and refine learning
- Programmed learning, engineered classroom responsible to maintain setting, reinforcement, individualization

The Philosophies: Religious

Now that the secular philosophies of education have been briefly discussed, we will turn our attention to a few religious philosophies of education. As mentioned in the history section, several key models are utilized in various Christian educational settings. In *Models of Religious Education*, Harold Burgess gives an excellent overview of the various Christian models, and it is from his book that most of the information of this brief section is based.

The Historic Prototype

According to Burgess, the Historic Prototype has four main areas of emphasis. "1) that religious education is fundamentally concerned with communicating a divinely given message; 2) that aims and subject matter are best ascertained from the Bible and from carefully preserved doctrines rooted in it; 3) that the teacher's role is to communicate the spirit and facts of the saving message as well as to assist the learner's assimilation into the church; and 4) that learners will live out the implications of the message with respect to their participation in the church" (Burgess 26). Leading individuals, both past and present, who adhere to this model range from Clement of Alexandria (second century) to C. S. Lewis (twentieth century).

The Classical Liberal Model: A Theological Model

The Liberal/Theological model was primarily a reaction to the Historic Model. It emphasized the social realm over individual salvation and was tied to progressive models of education taught by Dewey. According to Burgess, "The liberal model of religious education is characterized by: 1) the position that theological constructs are open to continual change; 2) the conviction that religious education is essentially concerned with social and cultural reconstruction, not with individual salvation; 3) the view that the religion teacher's task is to create social consciousness, and to develop social living skills ... ; 4) the espoused doctrine that Christian personality and lifestyles arise from the development of latent personal and religious capacities ..." (Burgess 76).

Mid-Century Mainline: A Theological Model

The Mid-Century model is described by Burgess as a "transition for a 'this-worldly' to a decidedly 'God and Church' orientation" (Burgess 109). Like the model before, it too was primarily a reaction, or at least a re-working, of the model that came before it, in this case the Liberal model. Burgess describes it in the following manner: "Whereas the attention of the liberal model is rather narrowly centered upon social interaction, the attention of the mainline model is broadened so as to include a 'God who works'" (Burgess 109). The tenets of the Mid-Century model are: "1) Normative educational decisions are based on judgments informed by a wide range of twentieth-century theological expressions. ... 2) The broad aim is to establish individuals in a right relationship with God and then to educate them for socially responsible, intelligent, and adult religious living. 3) The teacher's task is regarded as one of entering into a communal relationship with learners for the express purpose of guiding them in their growth within themselves, toward God, and toward others. 4) The learner's spiritual life is most effectively fostered within the revelatory fellowship of the Church" (Burgess 111–112).

Many utilizing the Mainline model were largely influenced by Neo-orthodox theologians such as Karl Barth and Reinhold Niebuhr.

The Evangelical Model

As with the prior models, the Evangelical model is largely a reaction or clarification of the former models. It, as the name suggests, was largely an evangelical refinement of the educational process. Again, according to Burgess, the Evangelical model followed certain criteria: "1) Theological views derived from data thought to be received by authoritative revelation are normative for theory and practice. The Bible is the source of authoritative revelation ... 2) Both aim and content are fundamentally concerned with the transmission of a unique message derived from the facts of revelation. 3) The primary teaching task is to fully and faithfully transmit the message of the learners. 4) Learners will then live out the implications of the message with respect to Christian living and eternal destiny" (Burgess 150).

Many of the well-known evangelical educational leaders are found in this group, ranging from Frank Gaebelein, Kenneth Gangel, Roy Zuck, and Robert Pazmiño.

Social-Science Model

If the Liberal model can be said to have been influenced by the leading secular theorists of its day, so too we can see a correlation between the Social-Science model and leading secular models, emphasizing science and sociology. The tenets of the Social-Science model are as follows: 1) its commitment to empirical rather than to armchair [theoretical] methodology; 2) its orientation toward objective, quantitative treatment of data; 3) its emphasis upon understanding and predicting religious behavior on the basis of laws derived from empirically observed and verified phenomena; 4) its concentration on hypothesis making and testing as a means for identification and developing teaching practices by which desired religious behaviors may be reliably facilitated; and 5) its strong theory-practice linkage" (Burgess 187).

The Homeschool Model

Many Christian families are leaving schools at a rapid rate, both secular and private. This phenomenon is due to several reasons: academic, spiritual, financial, social, and the failure of educational institutions. Most of these families turn to homeschooling, co-op education, or charter schools. Though there is not a cohesive model of homeschooling (approaches range from Montessori-based models to Charlotte Mason-influenced schooling (1842–1923), there is a definite "voice" within the homeschool movement. Most homeschool movements tend to be biblically based. One such example is the Class Homeschools, an online homeschool group that offers parental support and models of education. Their tenets are as follows: biblical foundations (committed to an educational philosophy which is ... after Christ); biblical principles (teach within the framework of biblical authority: Triune God, Creation in Six Days, et cetera); the goal of education (to glorify and enjoy God, to fear and trust God, to reason according to a biblical worldview, to love and serve God and our neighbor) (www.homeschools.org).

Concluding Thoughts

As one can see, there are many "philosophies" and models of education, both religious and secular. Other models not discussed in a comprehensive fashion, such as Classical Christian, are largely hybrid philosophies, combining two or more of the models. (In the case of Classical Christian, it is a hybrid of the Historic and Evangelical models.) Some of these philosophies have fascinating and even biblical overtones; others are downright anti-Christian. The point of which I want the reader to take note is that most of the philosophies develop their mindset from an outside source—either secular thought or religious. Some of the religious models have biblical principles, but rarely utilize the Bible (method, words, types, examples, et cetera) as the framework. The model or philosophy may have biblical principles, but may neglect to foster a truly Christ-centered education paradigm.

I am not suggesting that having an outside model is bad; it is not. Nor am I suggesting that all the presented philosophy models are anti-biblical (though some are). Many times, having an outside reference point is a productive means by which to categorize a thought or sequence of thoughts.

What I am suggesting is that in developing a Christian philosophy of education, one must begin with Christ, and this is where we turn.

PART I

THE FOUNDATION

1

CHRIST-BASED PHILOSOPHY OF EDUCATION

"I am the way, and the truth, and the life."

John 14:6

It is sufficient to say that Jesus of Nazareth is the center of Christianity. Without *the* Jesus of Nazareth, there is no Christian faith, past or present. Specifically, for the Christian believer, the historical, objective reality of the person of Christ is of utmost importance: who Jesus is, what He taught, and the work He accomplished is central to an understanding of a Christian worldview. Simply put, for the Christian, Jesus is everything! The study of Jesus Christ should be the pinnacle of any academic or philosophical field of enquiry. Jesus, and the book that informs individuals about Himself, the Bible, should be paramount in setting frameworks and paradigms of reality. Whether it is in biblical studies, academic studies, devotional life, or the practical application thereof, Jesus (His message, life, and teaching), as portrayed in Scripture, needs to be addressed and expounded upon; it is upon Him that a worldview of existence is to be formed.

In this section, the subject of Christology will be applied to a biblical philosophy of Christian education. Why should the person of Christ be applied to education? Plainly put, the reason is because it is imperative that one understands how the person of Christ shapes not only the structure of classes and the "religious" element of school life, but the content and view of reality as expressed in the Christian faith. Put another way, the person of Christ must shape every aspect of a biblical philosophy of education, and ultimately all of life; who Jesus is must translate itself into the superstructure of a Christian organization, school, or otherwise.

In order to demonstrate how Christology relates to a biblical philosophy of education, the terms *Christology* and *Philosophy* need to be defined and then related to the person of Christ as the basis for which objective reality exists within a Christian philosophy of education. Specifically, a discussion of the effects of biblical, theological, and ethical frameworks of Christology on education will be viewed in light of Jesus' self-proclamation. The overall premise will be that without Christ, there can neither be a biblical philosophy of education nor a Christian worldview of reality; for in Him is truth, life, and the preeminence of God.

The Person of Christ

For in Christ all the fullness of the Deity lives in bodily form.

Colossians 2:9 NIV

According to Donald Bloesch, Christology "constitutes the heart of theology, since it focuses on God's work of salvation in the historical figure of Jesus of Nazareth and the bearing that this has on the history of humankind" (Bloesch 15). In its simplest form, Christology is the study of Christ. However, when the magnitude of who Jesus is comes to light, Christology is much more than a study. It is the eternal significance of God invading space and time; it is a penetrating insight into the plan and purpose of salvation and love; it is the reality that God became man and lived among us (Php 2).

On a practical level, Christology deals with several prophetic and metaphysical elements of Christ's person: His pre-incarnate state (Heb 10:7–10), His eternal state (Jn 1:1), His Sonship state (Ps 2), and the prophetic significance of Old Testament fulfillment. Likewise, Christology deals with the reality of His historical being: His virgin birth, His ministry and miracles, His teaching and message, His death, resurrection, and ascension into heaven. On a grander scale, Christology discusses the future and eternal reign of Christ: His pre-eminence and the mystery of His incarnation. Taken from a large vantage point, Christology encompasses eternity, though most of the ontological elements are unknown to humankind.

For the sake of clarity (and due to the largeness of the topic), three elements of Jesus' words concerning Himself will act as the basis of application towards a Christian philosophy of education. The three elements as spoken by Christ are the *way* (biblical truth, relating to the message and people), the *truth* (objective reality), and the *life* (sociology/ethics). These three words, and the conceptual meaning behind them, will be central to the discussion of Christology and a biblical philosophy of Christian education, and are part of the integration process of a Christ-based model of education.

Philosophy of Biblical Education

According to J. P. Moreland and William Lane Craig, philosophy "comes from two Greek words: *philein*, 'to love,' and *sophia*, 'wisdom.' Thus a philosophizer is a lover of wisdom. ... Accordingly, philosophy may be defined as the attempt to think rationally and critically about life's most important questions in order to obtain knowledge and wisdom about them" (Moreland and Craig 13). Utilizing this definition for biblical education, one could insert the word *biblical*, and get the following: "a biblical philosophy of education is an attempt to think rationally and critically about life's most important questions in order to obtain knowledge and wisdom about them." However, in order to stress the fullness of the biblical witness, it would be wise to end with a biblical disclaimer: The Bible, as God's inspired Word, is the basis and the objective foundation for obtaining knowledge and wisdom; it is from Scripture that the framework of reality exists, imparting its truth to all fields of enquiry and knowledge. Thus, its declaration shapes all educational pursuits.

Therefore, a biblical philosophy of education (using Moreland's and Craig's definition with my ending) would look something like this:

> A biblical philosophy of education is an attempt to think rationally and critically about life's most important questions in order to obtain knowledge and wisdom about them. The Bible, as God's inspired Word, is the basis and the objective foundation for obtaining knowledge and wisdom; it is from Scripture that the framework of reality exists; imparting its truth to all fields of enquiry and knowledge. Thus, its declaration shapes all educational pursuits.

Put another way, a biblical philosophy of education is one where the Bible shapes reality, therefore creating a biblical worldview of existence.

Christological Philosophy of Education

The question now arises, how does Christology shape a philosophy of education? The answer to this question, as hinted above, is to be found in Christ's words, "I am the *way*, the *truth*, and the *life*" (Jn 14:6). Here, three main elements of biblical integration are discovered.

First, by Christ proclaiming that He is "the way," Jesus has declared something that has biblical ramifications—for "the way" suggest a "path" or a "plan" that God has revealed for salvation. Jesus seems to be saying that there is a "way" of life, a course to be followed—He is it! Intrinsic within Christ's proclamation is the notion that a "way" has been foretold, or that there is a "path" that God has deemed acceptable. Essentially, Jesus is saying that He is the "path." God has a story to tell through providential history, a people to work through (both the Jew and the church), and a purpose to solidify.

Christ's radical declaration has immense biblical overtones; of which, on a primary level, is the suggestion that the Old Testament discusses the "plan" of Christ's coming. Inherent as well within this claim is the fact that Jesus is the "way" proclaimed prophetically by the writers of ancient Scripture; therefore, relegating divine authority is ascribed to the Old Testament Canon. In shortened verbiage, Jesus is proclaiming that God has told of a plan of salvation, perfectly so; and because He has communicated His will through Scripture, one can rest assured that Jesus is the "way" God has decreed; Jesus is God's plan! And since God and Christ declare Scripture as divinely inspired, it follows logically that Scripture not only informs individuals of Christ, but of objective reality, and therefore is the message for the ages in sequence, history, and reality. Christ is the "way" and Scripture upholds and teaches the "way" to God's people. So, not only is Jesus the "way" for salvation, He is also the "way" foretold in ages past, and "the way" for believers to follow.

Second, Jesus' proclamation that He is "the truth" reveals that God's "logos" (i.e. "logic" and "true utterance" or objective reality) is wrapped up in the person of Jesus. The word for "truth" in this passage of John is *aletheia*. According to Albert Barnes, *aletheia* means, "a representation of things as they are" (Barnes, E-Sword). So, truth, as spoken by Christ, means things that are "truly" true, objectively so; not merely a subjective truth. Subjectivism, remember, is the belief that one cannot know anything for sure because of differing experiences and viewpoints. Objective truth defends reason and empirical fact. It provides an intellectual foundation for verifiable standards of true "truth" and value. Jesus is saying that He is "objective reality"; He is the real thing!

The implications of "Christ as truth" in relation to the educational realm are vast. For on one hand, as Frank Gaebelein and Arthur Holmes have suggested, "All truth [objective reality] is God's truth" and therefore factually true (Gaebelein 20 and Holmes 17). As a result of being objectively and factually true, all reality is an open arena in which Christians can participate. As an example, Christians can partake as doctors, scientists, and artists because part of their "job" would be to discover the "truth" revealed about God in their particular field of enquiry. Scientists study God's handiwork and natural laws. Artists relate God's beauty, and pastors preach Christ and teach His Word (God's revealed truth), and so forth.

On the other hand, "truth" can also mean the direct, revelatory truth of God in Christ—Christ is "truly God"; in Christ is the fullness of God's "truth"! Either way, and in most cases inclusive to both, God in Christ has immense overtones—with overarching ramifications penetrating all subject areas, natural laws, scientific advancement, and ethical codes. Christ is indeed the truth of all things. Therefore, the worldview implication is that Christ, as truth, has an omniscient role in fact and in all objective reality; His person is preeminent in every nuance of universal and supernatural reality.

On a practical note, this means that all areas of objective (and even subjective critique and explanation) reality are at the disposal of a philosophy of Christian education because, in an ultimate sense, truth (objectively so) discovered from academic discourse is nothing more than a reflection of the truth of Christ, and therefore, appropriate for inclusion in a philosophy of education. However, as stated above, any claim of "truth" is to be shaped by God's Word. Any assertion of "truth" that supersedes Scripture is nothing more than speculation, rendering it subjective. Therefore, it must be discarded.

Christians are called to have the mind of Christ and to seek God's truth by attempting to think His thoughts (1Co 2:16). Through the revelation of His Son, Scripture (as inspired by the Holy Spirit), and the physical world, a Christian can participate in the quest to proclaim God's truth to a world in desperate need to hear it.

Likewise, Christians in the educational realm are called to present God's truth to their students, using the width and depth of Scripture; the universe is open game! God is the author of all that is, and we as His children are to seek His ways in all endeavors.

Third, Christ proclaims that He is "the life." Whereas "the way" suggests biblical fulfillment, "truth" reveals the objective reality of God, "life" suggests the ethical mores or code determined by God.

In other words, "the way" is the biblical foundation, "the truth" is the biblical and philosophical foundation, and "the life" is the ethical and Christian-living foundation. The "life" suggests a way of living. The word *life* has near and far ramifications. In one sense, it is "life" given to a soul, a salvific imputation. In another sense, it is a code of ethics, a new mode of living based upon a new, creational supernatural alignment (being born again); simply put, Christian living. Albert Barnes, in a discussion of "life" from the gospel of John, puts it as follows:

> The evangelist had just affirmed that by the λόγος Logos or "Word" the world was originally created. One part of that creation consisted "in breathing into man the breath of life." God is declared to be "life," or the "living" God, because he is the source or fountain of life. This attribute is here ascribed to Jesus Christ. He not merely made the material worlds, but he also gave "life." He was the agent by which the vegetable world became animated; by which brutes live; and by which man became a living soul, or was endowed with immortality. This was a "higher" proof that the "Word was God," than the creation of the material worlds; but there is another sense in which he was "life." The "new creation," or the renovation of man and his restoration from a state of sin, is often compared with the "first creation;" and as the Logos was the source of "life" then, so, in a similar but higher sense, he is the source of "life" to the soul dead in trespasses and sins.

It is with the dual nature of "life" that integration can occur within the concept of a Christ-based philosophy of Christian education. A biblical philosophy should include the "salvation" message of Christ as well as the moral implications of the saved life. In other words, because of the imputation of the Spirit bringing life, a Christian is to live and produce the fruit of life. Life begets life. Christ proclaims that, as Christians, we are to bear fruit. Christ fully understands that a life saved (regeneration) will, in effect, live a saved life (fruit of the Spirit). On the other hand, "life" can mean the pursuit of living according to God's purposes—living the "good life"; seeking God's beauty, truth, and goodness in the day-to-day walk with Him.

Any Christian academic or educational endeavor must consciously put before students' eyes the gospel message. The fact that a person must be born again is of eternal significance. On the same note, any understanding or impartation of a Christian worldview must encompass what it means to "live" the Christian life. What does a life filled with the Holy Spirit look like? What does it mean to act and seek after Christ? The "life" part of Jesus' tri-fold declaration is profoundly practical; it is where the rubber meets the road; it is the process of sanctification whereby the Holy Spirit continues to fashion believers into the image of Christ. The Christian "life" is precisely what Jesus said it should be for the believer: salt and light for a hurting (or "an unsaved") world. The point for this discussion in relation to life is that a Christological understanding of education must include the "living" element if it is to reflect the character and commands of Christ.

Putting Together a Christological and a Philosophical Mode of Christian Education

Based upon the overriding notion of Christ as "the way, the truth, and the life," and the biblical means of understanding the application of that statement in a form of Christian education, a christological and biblical philosophy of Christian education may best be summarized as follows:

1. A biblical and christological philosophy of Christian education should be a biblical endeavor. All elements of educational thought and subject are to be informed by, and through, the Bible. Instituting a biblical worldview is paramount to a christological and biblical philosophy of Christian education. Primary to the worldview is the understanding of Christ as the "way"—the scriptural foretelling and fulfillment of God's plan of salvation, as portrayed in the Bible, culminating in Christ.

2. A christological and biblical philosophy of education must integrate objective truth in all fields of inquiry. It must test all fact, findings, and information in light of the truth of the Bible, God's

objective Word. Of primary concern is the centrality of Christ as "the truth" and *Logos* of God: truth revealed. Christ's person and plan, as expounded in the fullness of Scripture, should be considered in all subject areas and fields.

3. A christological and biblical philosophy of education must include the message of salvation and a moral code for living. It must determine that there is a "right" code and a "wrong" code of ethics—there is sin and there are consequences. Primary to this area is that Jesus is "life"; He is salvation and provides an abundant life when one abides in Him.

Final Thoughts Concerning Christ-based Education

As demonstrated in this brief discussion of Christ and education, the field of christological studies unquestionably shapes a biblical view of Christian education. A Christian philosophy of education must first be addressed in light of the person of Christ and His proclamation of who He says He is and the works He came to fulfill. One of the clearest declarations is the statement, "I am the way, the truth, and the life." With this proclamation, one finds the biblical, theological, and ethical framework for a christological philosophy of Christian education. Without Christ, or His claims found in the Bible, one could have neither a Christian philosophy of education, nor a Christian philosophy of anything.

Of course other grand disclosures of Jesus' person can shape a Christ-based philosophy of education. Notice the sampling:

- John 6:51: "**I am the living bread** which came down from heaven. If anyone eats of this bread, he will live forever."

- John 8:23: And He said to them, "You are from beneath; **I am from above**. You are of this world; I am not of this world."

- John 8:12: Then Jesus spoke to them again, saying, "**I am the light of the world**. He who follows Me shall not walk in darkness, but have the light of life."

- John 10:9: "**I am the door**. If anyone enters by Me, he will be saved, and will go in and out and find pasture."

- John 10:11: "**I am the good shepherd.** The good shepherd gives His life for the sheep."

- John 10:36: "Do you say of Him whom the Father sanctified and sent into the world, 'You are blaspheming,' because I said, '**I am the Son of God**'?"

- John 11:25: Jesus said to her, "**I am the resurrection and the life**. He who believes in Me, though he may die, he shall live."

- John 15:1: "**I am the true vine**, and My Father is the vine-dresser."

- John 19:21: Therefore the chief priests of the Jews said to Pilate, "Do not write, 'The King of the Jews,' but, 'He said, "**I am the King of the Jews**."'"

- Acts 7:32: Stephen speaking of Moses' encounter at the burning bush, "saying, '**I am the God of your fathers**—the God of Abraham, the God of Isaac, and the God of Jacob.' And Moses trembled and dared not look."

- Acts 9:5: And he said, "Who are You, Lord?" Then the Lord said, "**I am Jesus**, whom you are persecuting. It is hard for you to kick against the goads."

These declarations can, and do, add to the overall impact of the statement "I am the way, the truth, and the life." The totality of Jesus' claims testifies to the fact that He is the Alpha and Omega, the beginning and end to all areas of truth. In Him is found the truth of God!

2

EDUCATION: THE JESUS WAY

In order to understand a Christ-based philosophy of education, the person of Jesus must be studied and meditated upon; His declarations must be weighed and put into practice; His methods studied and replicated. The following sections will address all three areas. First, Jesus the student will be assessed by looking at the text in Luke 2:45–52. First, the question will be asked: How did Jesus learn. Second, in what environment? Third, Christ's teaching methods and educational directives will be examined in order to discover His priorities and to seek practical ways to apply them.

Jesus as Student

And it came to pass, that after three days they found him in the temple, sitting in the midst of the doctors, both hearing them, and asking them questions. And all that heard him were astonished at his understanding and answers. And when they saw him, they were amazed: and his mother said unto him, Son, why hast thou thus dealt with us? behold, thy father and I have sought thee sorrowing. And he said unto them, How is it that ye sought me? wist ye not that I must be about my Father's business? And they understood not the saying which he spake unto them. And he went down with them, and came to Nazareth, and was subject unto them: but his mother kept all these sayings in her heart. And Jesus increased in wisdom and stature, and in favour with God and man.

Luke 2:46–52 KJV

What is the aim of Christian education? According to Martin Luther (an early advocate of Christian education), a child is to be trained for the fullest possible participation in the kingdom of God. Luther advised, "Above everything else, bring up children in the fear and knowledge of God" (Bruce 213). Education reformer David Hicks states that the "end of education is not thinking; it is acting" (Hicks vi). Though Hicks, a Christian, may implicitly think "acting" is the end, the Christian educator must be more specific: the end of education is to "act" like Jesus, not in some theatrical, or even "noble" way, but in the molding of oneself after Him. The end must be to conform one's thoughts, actions, and motives into the image of Christ. Therefore, the supreme task of Christian education is to give students the opportunity to draw close to Jesus Christ, to live a life consistent with biblical truth, and to be conformed into His image by the power of the Holy Spirit. So, the aim of Christian education is Christ.

Taking a look at how Jesus lived is the best beginning. As an adolescent, Jesus grew in four specific ways: mentally, physically, spiritually, and socially. This picture of Jesus as a student, given in the second chapter of Luke, verses 40–52, shows us Christ in a learning environment. I believe we have been provided with this section of Scripture to guide us in the realm of educational pursuit. This portrait of Jesus' education experience gives us a model of a student, a basic classroom, and the results of instruction. It must be pointed out, however, that Jesus' spiritual wisdom didn't come from instruction (it came from above), though it was more clearly revealed in this question and answer format.

One of the important facets to recognize in studying this passage of Scripture is that Jesus had a mental faculty towards learning. In his excellent essay, *Jesus the Logician*, Dallas Willard says, "We need to understand that Jesus is a thinker, that this is not a dirty word but an essential work, and that His other attributes do not preclude thought, but only insure that He is certainly the greatest thinker of the human race" (Willard 4). Willard rightly points out that Jesus' genius was revealed even in His childhood found in Luke 2 (Willard 4). It is here that we turn.

The Student

The first thing we learn about Jesus in this portion of Scripture is that He was Spirit-led. The Holy Spirit played a pivotal role in His education. Verse 40 says that Jesus was "strong in spirit." He was led and filled with God's truth as inspired and taught by the Spirit Himself. Second, we learn that He was "filled with wisdom." His knowledge was based in the reality and truth of God. Though we do not know the specifics of what the Spirit was teaching Him, we can be sure it revealed the attributes of God's person and plan. Third, the "grace of God was upon Him." God's favor was leading Him. God had a purpose and goal for His Son.

The Classroom

One must not suppose that Jesus invented the following instructional methodology. He didn't. What is being established is that He worked largely within a Jewish form of education. In essence, Jesus was engaged in a model to be seen as a foundational element upon which one can build.

The second thing we learn of Jesus as a student is the type of classroom environment in which He was engaged. In verse 46, we see several important aspects of a good classroom atmosphere. First, Jesus was sitting in the midst of the teachers. He was engaged in the conversation. Implied here is student-teacher interaction. Second, Jesus was listening (Gr. *akouo*: to give audience, to understand). He undoubtedly was listening to what the teachers were saying and probably checking it against the truth of what the Holy Spirit was teaching Him.

Third, He was asking the teachers questions (Gr. *eperotao*: to ask for; to inquire, seek, or desire). It appears that He was interacting with the thoughts and propositions posed by the educators. Whether the teachers were giving correct information, we are not sure, but we do know the result of their teaching time with Jesus was that they were astonished. I think part of their astonishment came from Jesus' correct understanding of God and truth in general, and from the fact that one so young could be so wise. This is a excellent example of a classroom situation where the Holy Spirit influenced and led.

The Instruction

The final aspects we learn in relation to Spirit-led teaching are the results of the instruction that took place. In verse 52, we read that Jesus increased in wisdom (Gr. *sophia*: spiritual and earthly wisdom); stature (Gr. *helikia*: maturity); and in favor (Gr. *charis*: influence, grace) with God and man. This is holistic growth. Jesus' whole person grew as a result of teaching. He didn't just grow mentally, spiritually, or in any other independent way; His entire self grew. The result of Christian education ought to be ministry to the totality of the student. It is a comforting thought that the Lord loves all of me, and wants to redeem and use every nuance of my being—my physical strength (what I may have of it), my mental capacities (what little I have), my spiritual person (continually growing into His image), and my relationship with others. He wants every part of me to reflect Him. The purpose of Christian education should be to shape a person into the image of Christ, mentally, spiritually, socially, and physically.

Application

It is important to notice the holistic way Jesus grew. His person grew, and if Christian educators are to model their classrooms after Jesus, we too, must pursue a holistic approach, ensuring that a child is educated wholly.

Christian teachers, like Jesus, are to rely on the Holy Spirit to accomplish what the Lord would have in the lives of their students. Educators are to encourage their students to be open to the Holy Spirit as informed by Scripture, letting them know that God has a purpose for their lives. Teachers are to conduct a classroom or educational environment that engages the whole student—asking questions, probing for answers, challenging students with biblical truth, and sitting among the students, serving and ministering by whatever means possible. Finally, instructors have the privilege of watching the Holy Spirit accomplish His purposes in the lives of students. They can marvel when a student begins to grow spiritually, academically, socially, and physically. Teachers can give God the glory when their students begin to think, act, and live a little more like Jesus.

Educational and Rabbinical Methods

To give a more concise view of how Jesus learned, it is quite appropriate to look at the educational environment of His day. According to Packer, Tenney, and White, "The Israelites provided a well rounded education for their children. It included religious instruction as well as training in practical skills … it strove to impart not only knowledge but wisdom, centered around one's relationship with God" (Packer, Tenney, White 452). Included in this "well rounded education" was an emphasis on understanding the needs of the students (452), being fully versed in the subject being taught (452), and an understanding of parental responsibility (453). According to Michael J. Anthony, the Jewish educational framework "use[ed] the books of the Mosaic Law as a basis of the curriculum, they required boys to memorize large portions of the Law. Content also included mathematics and writing" (see Anthony 35).

Students in Jesus' day usually went to synagogue schools and also learned a vocation. Besides practical knowledge, great stress was placed on Scripture reading and memorization as well as music, etiquette, and warfare. Classes were usually four hours long on hot days and longer on cooler days. School was a year-round endeavor. Classes were age-integrated, and usually direct, individual attention was given to the students, whereby they could ask questions and dialogue with the teacher on matters of knowledge.

Alfred Edersheim believes that "there is clear evidence that Jesus was familiar with the art of writing, which was by no means so common in those days as reading" (Edersheim 111). Edersheim's reasoning is based upon the fact that Jesus may have known several languages (Hebrew, Assyrian, Hebrew, Phoenician), and makes a passing reference to the expression "one iota or one little hook" (Lk 16:17; Mt 5:18), which only applies to Hebrew. This knowledge, following Edersheim's logic, allows Jesus to translate or transpose Scripture from language to language. However, there is not a clear scriptural basis to presume that Jesus wrote extensively.

Much of Jesus' educational upbringing may have been intricately tied to the rabbinical method of instruction. Jewish rabbinical education was comprised of four main methods of instruction. (The acronym PaRDeS is used to remember the four methods.)

The first is *P'shat*. The Hebrew word *P'shat* means "simple." The *P'shat* method was used by rabbis to convey the literal and plain meaning of a text. *Remez* is the second method. The Hebrew word *Remez* means "to hint." The *Remez* method seeks deeper meaning than the *P'shat*; it looks between the lines and seeks deeper truth not revealed in the *P'shat*. Third is the *MiDrash*. The Hebrew word *MiDrash* means "to search." It seeks out allegorical and descriptive insight from the *P'shat* and *Remez*. The fourth and final method is the *Sod*. The Hebrew word *Sod* means "secret." Here the rabbi would reveal the secret meaning of a text, either hidden or unrevealed. This area of teaching usually verged on the mystical. The rabbinical teaching levels are not necessarily teaching strategies, but content-based applications and biblically informed methods of finding meaning and clarity in Old Testament Scripture. Incidentally, the Christian church has utilized four levels of meaning as well: literal or grammatical, allegorical or figurative, anagogic or mystical, and topological or moralizing (Gardner 81).

Though we have little information in Scripture directly stating a correlation, studying the teaching methods of Jesus shows that He may have been influenced by the various methods in His schooling. One can find literal meaning, allegorical meaning, application, mystery, et cetera in the scope of His teaching. Therefore, one can conclude that Jesus was inspired (by the Father) and influenced (by earthly teachers) to learn and teach in a formidable way.

A Continuity Between What the Bible Teaches, What Jesus Learned as a Student, and What He Taught as an Adult

As mentioned earlier, however, the New Testament is clear about the fact that Jesus grew in four distinct areas: wisdom, stature, His relationship with God, and His relationship with man. Likewise, as an adult, Jesus taught a similar theme: loving God with all one's heart, mind, and soul, and loving one's neighbor as oneself. In essence, how Jesus learned as a student (either from God, family, rabbis, or all three) was translated into what He taught as an adult. Jesus undoubtedly saw the deeper, whole-person approach of education as central to educational pursuits.

The fact that Jesus was a student of great significance should go uncontested. Not only does the Bible declare Him to be the very image of God, but His life, testimony, and ultimately, the resurrection, verify the claim. It is no wonder then that Jesus grew in accord with the divine plan of God—all aspects of His person were utilized and educated: His mental faculties, His physical person, His social maturity, and His spiritual life with His Father. His total person was shaped and molded according to God's plan. Jesus was, and is, the model student, and as such, is the ideal to which Christians should look, and is the example upon which we should base learning results.

Jesus as Teacher

The Teaching Strategies Found in the Gospel of Luke

If there is one aspect of Jesus' life and ministry that all Christians, and even non-Christians, agree upon, it is the fact that Jesus was a teacher. Not only was He called a teacher (rabbi), but the totality of His ministry was teaching the world about Himself. Jesus, unquestionably, had the greatest teaching ministry the world has ever seen! The Bible calls Jesus a teacher 45 times, and those who followed Jesus were called disciples (learners) 215 times (Garner 1).

His teaching techniques and methodologies were par-excellence. Jesus had an innate ability to communicate the greatest of truths in the simplest of terms. He taught lectures (Sermon on the Mount); used cooperative learning groups (a small group of disciples); was a master at higher order questioning ("Who do you say that I am?"); utilized object lessons (fig tree, woman at the well); was a master storyteller and sparked the imagination (parables); challenged His students ("go and do the same"); used proverbial expressions and absurdities ("camel through the eye of a needle"); taught ethics and moral virtue (Beatitudes); and most importantly, taught the people about God's plan for the world through Himself.

Many books have been written about Jesus, the teacher. In the 1920s, Herman Horne wrote several books dealing with Jesus the teacher, and more recently, Roy Zuck penned a book about Jesus' teaching style. Horne emphasized and analyzed Jesus' conversations, questions, parables, word pictures, modeling, and attitudes from the vantage point of one gleaning from Jesus' superior teaching techniques. Zuck utilized a similar format in that he looked at the methods of Christ's teaching. However, to get the fullest picture of Jesus the teacher, one must begin with the clearest book on Jesus' teaching techniques, the Bible.

The four Gospels offer a portrait of Jesus as a teacher, with each book contributing a unique perspective on His life, ministry, and teaching methodologies. Matthew seems to present Jesus as the promised Messiah, focusing upon His role as the Messianic King. Mark portrays Jesus as the anointed Servant, One who is doing the work of God from obedience to death to resurrection. John presents Jesus as the Incarnate Son, proclaiming the "Word became flesh" and the manifestation of this Word to the world. Luke presents Jesus as the universal Savior, a compassionate teacher of the lost and needy. The Gospels are at the same time independent from, and yet dependent upon one another. Independent in that each author paints a clear and concise picture of Jesus, with an intended purpose and readership. Each gospel can stand alone and still give the reader a clear idea of who Jesus was and what He accomplished. The Gospels are dependent upon one another in that, when read as a whole, the complete picture of Jesus as Prophet, Priest, King, Servant, Teacher, et cetera, is drawn. If one wants to understand the fullness of who Jesus was and what He accomplished, all four Gospels are necessary. However, it is the unique story that the Holy Spirit inspired the authors to tell that offers a glimpse into a particular aspect of Jesus' life and ministry.

Based on the premise that a unique picture of Jesus appears in each of the Gospels, I have chosen to focus in on the gospel of Luke. Though Jesus' teaching methods are found throughout the four Gospels, Luke seems to highlight the specific traits of Jesus as teacher in a very "teacher friendly" manner. The variety of teaching tactics used by Jesus are clearly defined and easily grasped within the context of the Luke's gospel. Robert Pazmiño rightly deems the gospel of Luke as "Methods from the Master Teacher" (Pazmiño 36).

For the sake of simplification, this discussion will be limited to the first seven chapters of the gospel of Luke, highlighting various teaching elements found within the book. (Appendix A offers an overview of techniques found throughout the entire book of Luke.) I have focused on these chapters as a means of demonstrating how one can approach the Bible with "teacher lenses." My intent is to demonstrate an instructional pattern in Jesus' life and ministry. However, a complete investigation would indicate that the entire gospel of Luke clearly shows Jesus as a Master Teacher.

My approach in this section is more chronological and practical than expositional or topical. My intention is not to become tied up in word studies or interpretive procedures; rather, I will look for principles and applications that can be drawn from the text and applied to the educational realm. Simply put, I will be using the principles bestowed by Luke for application and modeling rather than for doctrinal concern.[1]

---

[1] *Background*

The author of the gospel of Luke is not stated in the text of the book. However, tradition and internal evidence support Luke as the author (Jensen 157).

Chapters One through Three

Chapters one through three do not specifically involve Jesus as a teacher. The reason is simple: Jesus was just a lad (being born and raised); He hadn't officially begun His teaching ministry. However, this does not mean that the first three chapters of Luke have little to tell us about education. On the contrary, they give us great principles to apply, especially on the philosophical foundation upon which Christian education rests.

Chapter One

In chapter one, Luke gives the reader an introduction and then proceeds to explain the announcement and birth of John the Baptist. Gabriel visits Mary and explains the supernatural way by which she will conceive. Also in chapter one, Mary and Zacharias set forth some of the most sublime verses in the Bible; in essence, they worship the Lord in word and song. There is a grand anticipation and preparation resounding in chapter one; it sets the stage for the excitement to come.

Background cont.

The book was the first in a two-part series (Luke and Acts) dedicated to a Roman government official named Theophilus. The writing style (grammar, et cetera) is very academic, and the insights given by the author concerning disease, vocabulary, and the details of geography and cultural life point to an educated and informed writer. Luke was a traveling companion of Paul and a gentile convert to the Christian faith (Barclay 1). By profession, Luke was a doctor (Col 4:14) and may have been the physician on one of the ships upon which Paul sailed (Morgan 10). His relationship with Paul seemed to be close. He is mentioned by Paul in a few of his letters and may have been with the apostle up until his martyrdom (Morris 1082). Scholars debate as to the exact date of its writing, but many put it at circa AD 60. The main theme of the Gospel is that of the universal Savior (Colquhoun 42) committed to "seek and to save that which was lost" (Lk 19:10). However, several key areas of emphasis are given throughout the book: Son of Man among men (Lk 19:10); the perfect God-man (Lk 1:35); and, the salvation of God (Lk 3:6), among others (Jensen 159).

The Christian educational principles drawn from the chapter are as follows: first, as Jesus was the "center" of the conversation, the One for whom all were preparing, so too, He should be the "center" of all educational endeavors. The historical reality of Christ and the theological ramifications of His coming are essential to any understanding of truth. Since Christ is truth, the multiplicity of who He is should transcend all areas of educational inquiry, be it history, science, or math. God's truth is wrapped up in Christ.

The second principle is that worship (man's adoration and exultation of God) is an essential component to any educational model. Man is not the "thinking man"; rather, man is the "worshiping man." Humanity was created to worship God. Sin and rebellion have caused many to worship false gods, but through Christ, true worship has been instituted. In Christ, worship is in "spirit and truth" (Jn 4:23). Therefore, worship is the pinnacle of the Christian's existence and should be a focal point in any educational setting.

The third principle is that words are a crucial aspect to education. Mary spoke her prayer/poem to the Lord; Zacharias sang words in praise of what the Lord had done. In an ultimate sense, Christ is the Word Incarnate; He is God in bodily form. God communicates to humanity through words—Christ, the Bible, prophecy, and so on. Words are essential! Therefore, words need to be an important part of any educational model. On a specific level, the Word of God should be at the forefront. But on a lesser level, the telling of stories, the reading of books, the recitation of poetry and hymns, and the transference of information through words all need to be an intricate aspect of Christian education. Additionally, the introduction of language, both foreign and native, must play an important role in the early stages of educational life.

Chapter Two

In chapter two, Luke proclaims the birth of Jesus, the visitation of the shepherds, the blessing of Simeon and Anna, and the story of Jesus as a student in the temple. As in chapter one, focus is given to worship and thanksgiving—in this case specifically towards Jesus—pointing once again to the primacy of worship. However, the interesting educational principle drawn from chapter two is that of Jesus as a student. When Jesus was twelve years old, He tarried behind in Jerusalem to attend an "educational session" at the temple. He sat in the midst of the teachers, listening and asking questions. The result of His conversation with the teachers was that the instructors were astonished. Luke goes on to explain that Jesus grew in wisdom, stature, and favor with God and man. As mentioned in the section on Jesus as a student, there are several key components that are essential to understand in this passage, and very applicable towards principles of education.

Jesus modeled the basics of a learning environment. First, Jesus was sitting among the teachers. He was interacting. He was engulfed and engaged. This should be the model for students and teachers alike. Sit among one another, challenge, discuss, and engage one another. Second, Jesus was listening. His time with the teachers wasn't a monopoly. He listened to what they said; He didn't just talk at them. This tells us that the classroom environment was free from distractions and Jesus was able to listen. Likewise, classrooms of today should be disciplined and free from distractions. Teachers should learn the subtle art of classroom control. Third, Jesus was asking questions. He undoubtedly was asking questions based on the information the teachers had given Him. He was probably engaging the teacher so that truth would be known. Likewise, a classroom is one where teachers need to encourage questions, and students need to be taught how to ask questions. Classrooms need to be a forum where a teacher can inspire a student to want to know more. Education should, at times, be likened to a conversation, not a stern lecture.

Chapter Three

Chapter three begins with the ministry of John the Baptist—the baptism and preparation of Jesus—and concludes with the genealogy of Joseph. Several important educational principles can be derived from this section.

First, preparation is essential. John prepared the way for Jesus. Jesus was baptized and prepared Himself for His mission on earth. Likewise, teachers, students, and staff are to prepare themselves for their tasks. "Shooting from the hip" is not only sloppy, but ultimately a character flaw that allows poor preparation, and possibly misinformation to be the rule rather than the exception.

Second, as John preached repentance, so too, every teacher and student should understand that all people are in need of salvation and repentance. None is perfect. Mistakes will happen; projects get lost or are incomplete; lies are told, and so on. The fact is that people are sinners, and when sin occurs, repentance is needed. Humility and grace should be a cornerstone in all educational settings.

The third principle is that history is important. Luke, as inspired by the Holy Spirit, recorded an important aspect of Jesus' history. He was of the lineage of David and the implications of His history point to Him being the Messiah. History is important because it is God's unfolding tale. History should be taught, studied, and learned in each level of school. Moses, in his writings, declared the importance of remembering; Stephen, the martyr, told of God's wonders throughout history; so too should today's students remember and study what the Lord has done. Students should learn the chronological path upon which the Lord has set history in motion. Chronology is important in that it reminds us that there was a beginning, there is middle, and there will be an end. Today's progressive educators have tried to make history a "social science"; they have taken the sacredness of providence and turned it into a study of man's doings. Christian educators must rescue progressive attempts to strip history of its providential nature, and declare it for what it is: "His Story." I thoroughly believe that when teaching history, a chronological approach accomplishes this goal.

Chapters Four through Six

Beginning in chapter four, Jesus' ministry is well on its way. By now, Jesus has obviously been born, circumcised, educated, and has learned a trade (the subject of learning a trade deserves a discussion of its own). Presumably, He has also been brought up in a traditional Jewish household. Adulthood is upon Him, with the redemption of the world before Him. It is in the beginning of the fourth chapter that the teaching ministry of Jesus is clearly seen and defined.

Chapter Four

In chapter four, Luke tells of Jesus' temptations and use of Scripture, His public reading, the rejection by His hometown concerning His Messiah-ship, and the beginning of His miracles.

Educationally, several important principles can be found in this section. First, Jesus used Scripture to battle temptation. The use of Scripture has two key points. One, it points to the fact that Scripture is important in the battles of life. Scripture should be used to fight temptation as well as answer the questions of existence. Jesus had Scripture memorized, stressing the importance of internalizing God's Word; truth was a part of Jesus' person. Likewise, the Christian educator needs to rely upon Scripture in all areas of life and thought. Educators need to stress memorization (especially in the early years) of God's Word and pertinent facts (grammar rules, multiplication, et cetera) that will assist the child in the course of life.

Second, Jesus read Scripture aloud. Open reading is an important facet of any educational endeavor. Children learn confidence and gain better reading skills when reading is done aloud. Additionally, open reading will lead to open communication such as public speaking, which is a vital component of a well-rounded education.

Third, Jesus began His healing ministry. Though many individuals do not have the gift of healing, the principle drawn here is one of compassion. Teachers need to exude compassion for their students. Educators must attempt to see things through the eyes of a struggling or hurting student. In order to educate effectively, teachers must communicate deep love and compassion for their students.

Chapter Five

In chapter five, Luke writes of Jesus' miracles, His healings, the calling of Levi, and the beginning of His parables.

The miracle of the great catch in verses 1–11 demonstrates how Jesus taught His disciples through their failures. Even though the disciples didn't accomplish what they set out to do (catch fish), Jesus uses this failure to teach them a valuable lesson: they will be fishers of men. In the same manner, teachers are called to teach students through failure. One of the best ways to learn something is to fail at it. Rather than condemning and ridiculing a student, a teacher should bring them through the process, showing them the desired result, and ultimately leading them to success or a lesson learned from the failure.

In the calling of Levi, Jesus demonstrates that man's plans are not God's plans. Levi, a tax collector, had his own plan for life—to make money. However, Jesus had other plans for him. He reached out to the sinner and changed Levi's life forever. Likewise, teachers are always to remind students to seek the things of the Lord before their own plans. A student may yearn to be a sports star; God may want a doctor. One may want to be a lawyer; God may want a mother and a wife. Always encourage students to "seek first the kingdom of God and His righteousness" (Mt 6:33).

Jesus' use of parables in verses 33–39 communicates several important principles. First, stories are important. People relate to stories, especially when they apply to themselves and are understood in the context of their lives. Teachers need to continually read stories and apply them to their students' lives. Fiction biography, among other genres of literature, has essential "stories" that students will benefit from. Parables use metaphor, simile, hyperbole, and other high-order thinking literary devices. In short, parables and stories cause students to think and apply the situation to their own lives. In the same manner, teachers need to use metaphor, simile, and other such literary devices to create an environment of creative thinking. Teachers are called to spark the imagination and transform the heart.

Chapter Six

In chapter six, Luke writes of Jesus' teaching on the Sabbath, His healing of a deformed hand, the choosing of His disciples, and His teaching regarding kingdom living (Sermon on the Plain).

Of the several important principles learned from the Sabbath, one that directly applies to the teacher is the need of rest, both for the teacher and for students (if the Lord rested on the seventh day, so too should man). Students need to rest from their labors. A day continually filled with brainwork may be more unproductive than one knows. Students need to mentally adjust, stretch, and relax their mental faculties. They need to rest and recoup. The brain is like a muscle. Working out a muscle day after day without breaks isn't as effective as working a muscle, then resting the muscle, then working it, then resting it, and so on. The work/rest principle makes for a stronger muscle and a "stronger" brain.

In verse 12, Luke tells us that Jesus Himself went out into the mountains to pray. For the teacher, rest and prayer are also essential. When one is giving of oneself day after day, only rest, silence, and prayer can satisfy. Silence in the life of a teacher is of great importance. Teachers need to regroup, bring their concerns before the Lord, and sit to hear from Him. Prayer, rest, and silence before the Lord should be part of a classroom's daily routine, and more specifically, part of the teacher's daily life.

Ah, the lecture! The "good 'ol" lecture enters the picture in verses 20–49. Jesus used lectures as one of His teaching methods. But note, Jesus didn't exclusively use lectures; they were a part of His arsenal, not the complete cadre of weaponry. Likewise, teachers need to lecture, especially when teaching large groups or communicating essential aspects of a lesson to the group, but lectures are not to be their only weapon either. Note that it took five chapters before group lectures entered the picture; Jesus utilized other teaching opportunities to strengthen His lecture. So too should teachers.

Chapter Seven

In chapter seven, Luke writes about the centurion's faith, the widow's son, Jesus' teaching on faith, Jesus' thoughts on John the Baptist, and the anointing of Jesus' feet.

In verses 1–9, Luke discusses the healing of the centurion's son. Here, not only do we get a glimpse of the faith portrayed by the centurion and the compassion showed by Jesus, but we also get a picture of Jesus listening to a man. Jesus listened diligently to the centurion's story, and then used the centurion as an example from whom others could learn. In essence, Jesus used this as a "teaching moment." He used a real life story to teach about faith and truth. Likewise, teachers are to use "teaching moments" to penetrate the lives of students. Teachers are to look for opportunities to hear the students out, listening diligently, and then comment briefly to exemplify or highlight the "moral" or theme of the student's story.

The second teaching element found in chapter seven is found in verses 18–23. Luke records how Jesus told John's disciples not to lose faith. Not only does Jesus use Scripture to uphold His teaching, but this passage also shows Him answering a question in an abstract fashion. He doesn't just say, "Yes, I am He"; rather, He causes them to think scripturally and abstractly. He causes the learners to make a correlation between what He is saying and what He did. He led them to the answer; He didn't just tell them the answer. This is higher-ordered thinking. Additionally, He uses the person of John the Baptist as an object lesson to teach the disciples about John's position as "forerunner." Jesus takes the question asked and turns it into a lesson for His students.

Again, the principles exuded by Jesus are very applicable to teaching. First, teachers are to utilize higher-ordered questioning and thinking. Giving a straight answer is not always the best way. Leading students and causing them to think is of utmost importance. As mentioned above, Jesus used a teaching moment to teach a truth, so too should teachers. Jesus also used parables to teach about faith.

Stories are essential elements of any teaching technique. Stories, fiction or non-fiction, should be used in all academic endeavors.

Conclusion

Through this brief analysis of chapters one through seven, it is evident that Jesus used various teaching methods to instruct people. A more thorough investigation of all the chapters would demonstrate the amazing way in which Jesus was able to communicate the truths of His message. According to Les Nixon, several key facets are found in Jesus' teaching methods.

First, Jesus used symbolism. Symbolism, as defined by Nixon, "explains one thing by comparing it to another" (L. Nixon 2). In the gospel of Luke, Jesus uses symbolism in His Sermon on the Plain. For example, He talks about "good fruit, bad fruit," and having a "mote in the eye."

Second, Jesus used the compare-and-contrast method. He compared one thing to another. In the gospel of Luke this is best seen in His parables: comparing a seed to the Word of God or a lamp to the light of a Christian's life (L. Nixon 3).

Third, Jesus used concise stories and parables. Throughout the gospel of Luke, Jesus utilized parables to teach the deep truth of God and life. Parables such as the Good Samaritan (ch. 10) and the Shrewd Accountant (ch. 16) are renowned in their style and impact (L. Nixon 4).

Fourth, Jesus used logic and reason. Clifford Wilson notes that "the events in Jesus' story of Lazarus and the Rich Man (Lk 16) follow each other clearly and in a logical pattern ... hearers had no trouble in following the events and drawing conclusions Jesus intended" (L. Nixon 6).

Fifth, Jesus used plot, climax, and resolution. Again, in the story of Lazarus, one can sense the plot (Lazarus vs. the rich man), the climax (the rich man watching Lazarus), and the climax resolution (the teaching and moral resolution to the parable).

Sixth, Jesus used poetry, including such elements as parallelism (truth conveyed in couplets, triplets, and so on; the Beatitudes in Lk 6:20–26); synonymous parallelism (each line expresses the same truth but in a different way: "He that is not with me is against me: and he that gathereth not with me scattereth." Lk 11:23, KJV); antithetic parallelism (succeeding lines express opposite truth: "He that finds life shall lose it; he that loses his life for my sake shall find it"); and step parallelism (development in each successive line) (L. Nixon 8).

Seventh, Jesus used metaphor (a word picture whereby something is described by calling it something else); simile (a word picture in which one thing is likened to another usually by the use of *as* or *like*); hyperbole (where a moral is taught by vivid imagery or overstatement); analogy (a relation of likeness between two things); and allegory (a form of speech in which the spiritual meaning of the story is woven into the telling of the story) (L. Nixon 8–10).

Eighth, Jesus used humor. Elton Trueblood, in his book, *The Humor of Christ*, discusses Christ's use of humor in parables and teaching, emphasizing the cultural contexts of sayings such as a "camel through the eye of a needle."

Another way of looking at the Lord as a teacher, especially as revealed in the gospel of Luke, is to look at His teaching thematically. In a thematic presentation, several key components arise. The themes below are not only beneficial for the professional school teacher, but all who profess Jesus as Lord and Savior; for in essence, we are all teachers of God's love for humankind.

Some of Christ's "teacher" qualities include (Yount 1):

- Agape leadership
- Self-discipline
- Forgiveness and patience
- Giving of self and a servant's heart
- A man of prayer and evangelism

- Had purpose and drive
- Used a variety of "teaching techniques" (parables, sermons, small groups) to communicate the truth
- Knew when to discipline and when to disciple
- Pointed others to greater things (namely, Himself)

Howard Hendricks, in the book *Christian Educator's Handbook* (19–25), discusses several key elements of Jesus' teaching style:

- Jesus was congruent
- Jesus was reality oriented
- Jesus was relational
- His message was relevant
- His message was authoritative
- His motive was love
- His motive was acceptance
- Jesus had a motive of affirmation
- His teaching was creative
- His teaching was unique
- His teaching was engaging
- His teaching was developmental

Robert Pazmiño, in his book *Foundational Issues in Christian Education* (37–38), stresses the following elements in Jesus' teaching as found in the gospel of Luke:

- Key Components: Open inquiry, correction, role modeling, and the need for response
- Jesus' Approach: Asks questions, listens, and exhorts disciples to open the Scripture
- General Principles: Teaching was authoritative; Jesus sought to have persons think for themselves; Jesus lived what He taught; Jesus loved those He taught; Jesus used mainly oral

instruction; His teaching was occasional in nature; it was adaptive to His audience; and included a variety of elements

These, of course, are just the tip of the iceberg. One could spend years digging into the depths of the Bible, studying Jesus and His purposes. Yet, one thing is clear: as Christians, we are to be like Him. He is our Lord and teacher! We are called to listen, to obey, and to ponder His words, thoughts, ideas, and vision. And just as important, we are to communicate His profound truth to a world in need; we are called to be teachers, to learn from Jesus, and to teach the world of His deeds.

Much more could be said relating to Jesus' teaching techniques, and many have written about the different facets of Jesus as a teacher. Appendix A lists some of the main facets of Jesus' teaching ministry found within the gospel of Luke.

3

DIGGING DEEPER: THE SERMON ON THE PLAIN

*And it came to pass also on another Sabbath, that he entered into
the synagogue and taught.*

Luke 6:6a KJV

As seen in the last section, Jesus was a teacher par-excellence! His
teaching strategies, educational goals (to teach of Himself and the
kingdom of God), and methodologies are unparalleled. Descriptions
of Jesus such as: "Rabbi" (Jn 1:38); and "a teacher come from God"
(Jn 3:2), along with the fact that Jesus had students or disciples
(learners), are prominent throughout Scripture and provide evidence
of His superior quality as a teacher. Unquestionably, the Bible portrays
Jesus as the Master Teacher!

In this section of the discourse, attempts will be made to analyze
one of Jesus' lessons or "teaching moments." Specifically, a detailed
study of Luke 6:20–49 will be the focus of analysis. This portion of
Luke is sometimes called the Sermon on the Plain.[1]

---

[1] *Background*

Scholars differ in opinion as to whether Luke 6:20–49 is an "abbreviated

To help understand this particular segment of Scripture and study it in light of its inherent teaching methodologies, several elements will be discussed. First, the context of the Scripture will be given. Second, the teaching environment will be taken into account. Third, specific teaching techniques used in the sermon will be analyzed. Finally, the morality and ethics of the sermon will be assessed. In short, this section will address the background, environment, techniques, and ethics (what I call nurture) of Luke 6:20–49, and apply several of the general principles found above by focusing in on a "lesson" taught by Jesus.

Context

The immediate context of the Luke 6:20–49 comes on the heels of prayer (Lk 6:12) and Jesus' choosing of the twelve disciples (Lk 6:13–16). Once Jesus has heard from the Father and chosen the twelve, He delivers the message amidst a multitude of people wanting to hear Him, to be healed, and to touch Him (Lk 6:17–19). It is among the seeming chaos that Jesus "lifted up His eyes ... and said ..." (Lk 6:20).

Environment

The environment in which Jesus taught is an interesting component of His ministry. It seems to fly in the face of conventional thought. Jesus taught with multitudes of people surrounding Him (Lk 6:19),

---

Background cont.

form of the same sermon as that recorded in Matthew 5–7" (Halley 500) (see Barnes and Henry), or a different sermon given with similar content. I believe the latter to be the case. For one, the geography is different. In Matthew, Jesus went up into the mountain; in Luke, He came down into the plain. Likewise, the wording and the parables used in both sermons, though similar in context, are different enough to conclude that Jesus probably gave two different messages (and possibly more that were not recorded) with comparable content (it is not uncommon for a person to give a similar message in various places). Finally, the intended audience is different. In as well as in small groups (Lk 24), and probably in every type of setting in between. He was followed, touched, harassed (usually by religious leaders), questioned (Jn 3), challenged on more than one account, and threatened. In short, His teaching environment was not without distraction. However, He was able to pronounce the noblest and most supreme truths the world has ever heard. His teaching seemed to be unaffected by the poor surroundings (His students didn't sit in rows and raise their hands when they wanted to ask questions), and Jesus was able to communicate truths that transformed His audience. I liken Jesus' teaching environment to that of a kindergarten class: students everywhere, doing their own thing, touching, hitting, learning the ropes of how to act "properly" in a formal setting.

The environment described by Luke establishes the fact that Jesus did teach amidst hostile circumstances not conducive to detailed instruction. However, because of His teaching methods (as described in chapter two), He was able to captivate His listeners and bring them to the point of learning profound truth.

In this particular portion of Scripture, after Jesus had finished praying and choosing the twelve disciples, they came down from the mountain to where the people were—in the plain—and it is at this point (interestingly, a low point) that all havoc broke loose. First, a great multitude from various places descended upon Him (v. 17). Second, many were vexed (troubled) and possessed (v. 18). Third, many came to be healed of diseases (v. 19). This was not a seminar

---

Background cont.

Matthew, the Sermon on the Mount was directed towards His disciples (Mt 5:1–2), whereas Luke suggests that Jesus addresses the whole multitude (v. 19) and His disciples (v. 20) (Morris 1094).

The exact location of the sermon is not known. Some scholars have suggested Capernaum (Packer, Tenney, White 515), though a concrete and specific place is lacking evidential support.

The narrative format, as suggested by Craig Keener, consists of segments of ethical teachings delivered as "blessings and woes"—a common form

on positive thinking, with people yearning to learn from an eloquent speaker. This was reality, and Jesus seemed to be communicating to His newly appointed disciples, "See the brokenness of the world. Look at the needs. Take note. To minister and proclaim is now part of your mission as My students." The environment in which Jesus ministered was a teaching tool in and of itself. Jesus used the circumstances to teach a lesson to His students. The setting may not have been perfect, but the Messenger (Jesus) was, and the message He gave was able to transcend it.

As teachers, we are to seek an ideal learning environment, yet we must always be aware of the reality of the world and the problems it poses to education. Christian teachers may sometimes feel as though the "multitudes are pressing in" as they are teaching. Events, students, and situations may not be ideal, and the problems that loom are distressful and dire. In all truth, there really is not a "perfect" teaching environment. But the reality of what Jesus was experiencing should resonate with all people, not just teachers. The world and the events that take place within it are imperfect. Likewise, teachers should remember that there will never be a "perfect" classroom or a "perfect" student. However, Jesus demonstrates that eternal truth can be communicated amidst the chaos; even in the place where one may throw up their hands and cry, "I give up!" teachers can make inroads and impart lifelong values. A good environment is ideal, but not essential. Jesus gives insight into how to turn a poor learning environment into a classroom for eternity.

Background cont.

of Jewish literary engagement (Keener 204). Robert Barclay believes that Jesus is more original in His approach than following the common teaching devices of His day. He says that Jesus' sermon is a "series of bombshells ... revolutionary ... quite unlike the laws which a philosopher or typical wise man might lay down" (Barclay 76).

The intent of the sermon seems to be to teach the ethics of the kingdom of God to the multitudes and to bring application and insight for living a life consistent with God's will for humankind. It has strong resemblance

[More] Technique

So, how did Jesus turn a poor learning environment into a classroom for eternity? The answer lies in the strategies He used to communicate the eternal. Jesus was able to touch lives amidst the chaos because He was the Master Teacher, and the way in which He taught reflected the unique and focused skill of a master artist. With people as the canvas and Jesus as the artist, we find His teaching to be the medium by which He touched the lives of those He was with two thousand years ago (and those who abide with Him today). The first thing one sees when looking at Luke 6 is the variety of teaching techniques Jesus used. He wasn't a one-tune jukebox. He was a record store! He used an amazing assortment of techniques in a short period of time.

He Lifted Up His Eyes Toward His Disciples

Verse 20 tells us that Jesus looked at His students, in this case the disciples and the multitude around Him. Eye contact is essential. It conveys personal attention and lets students know that what you are saying is directed at them.

Parallelism

Next, Jesus begins with parallelism; specifically, antithetical parallelism. We know this section as the "Beatitudes," yet it can also be seen as a type of Hebrew poetry where Jesus explains positive

---

Background cont.

to Moses' coming down from the mountain to give the Law. In this case, Jesus came down the mountain (after praying) and delivered the message to the people (Lk 6:12–17). I believe that this rendering of the message in Luke is truncated because it is addressed to the multitudes, and thereby gives principles for abiding in the kingdom to a wider audience; whereas in Matthew (Mt 5:1-2), the sermon is much longer and seems to be directed towards the disciples, with greater application and focused insight. The first is wider and condensed (Lk 6), the latter is specific and expanded. However, the intent is the same—the teaching of ethics and morals.

statements (vv. 20–23), and then gives the opposite (antithetical) in verses 24–26.

Compare and Contrast

Not only do the Beatitudes exemplify the use of parallelism, they also compare and contrast elements. Jesus compares the positive actions and behaviors to the negative. This, as mentioned in the background footnote, is a type of "blessings and woes" found in Hebrew literature. It is an effective teaching tool in that it communicates the oracles of God in both an affirmative and negative manner.

Challenges and Encourages

Good teachers both challenge and encourage students. Like athletic trainers, teachers should push and motivate students to move beyond their present stage. Laurence O. Richards and Gary J. Bredfeldt say, "Education is based upon an assumption that what is learned in the classroom can and should be applied outside the classroom" (Richards and Bredfeldt 113). In verses 20–49, Jesus models for us a teacher who challenges and encourages His students to apply what they have learned in the halls of life, not just in the halls of a classroom. In this portion of Scripture, we see a teacher who not only yearns to communicate and teach, but to have students apply what is being taught. Jesus challenges and encourages them to live the life He is teaching.

Jesus' words of challenge include: "But I say to you" (v. 27), in essence saying, "You have heard it the wrong way, now let Me clarify the right way"; "Can the blind lead the blind?" (v. 39), which is a rhetorical challenge; "Why do you call Me 'Lord, Lord,' and do not the things which I say?" (v. 46). Additionally, Jesus uses action verbs—words that command, such as bless (v. 28), offer (v. 29), give (v. 30), love (v. 35), bestow mercy (v. 36), judge not (v. 37), and so on.

In the same manner, Jesus uses words that encourage His students. Challenge without encouragement can bring despair. If an athlete's body is pushed constantly without rest, sickness and injury can be the result. The same is true in the educational realm. If a student is constantly challenged without encouragement, mental and emotional injury can be the outcome. Jesus used words of encouragement such as: blessed (vv. 20–23), rejoice (v. 23), love (v. 27), and do good (v. 35).

Parables

Most people love a good story. Christians are no exception. If one thing can be said about Jesus, it is that He has left with us some of the greatest stories and parables imaginable. Jesus used stories to communicate the deeper truths of God in a format that was both engaging and entertaining. He drew people in with His insights and characters (the prodigal son, a certain rich man). He was able to describe the momentous truths of God using the smallest of items (mustard seed, vines). And He was able to use the medium of stories to discuss the eternal.

In Luke 6:20–49, Jesus used a parable to teach and to draw the attention of His students to the truth He wanted them to learn. In verse 39, Jesus told the parable of the blind man. The moral of the story was to teach about judgment and sin, but the way in which Jesus told it allowed the listeners to associate with the character (the blind man) and apply the moral to their own life.

Analogy

In a similar fashion to parables, Jesus used analogies to communicate the deeper truths of God. He often compared a physical item to a truth of God. In verse 43, Jesus makes the analogy of a tree producing good fruit to a life that is to do the same. In verse 46, Jesus draws the following analogy: Living a life built on the foundation of God's Word is like building one's house on a rock, while living a life not grounded in God's Word is like building one's house upon sand.

The bottom line is that Jesus drew parallels in the guise of analogy in a striking and very effective manner.

Asking Questions

Not only was Jesus the master storyteller and analogy giver, He was a crafted question asker. He used many forms of questions throughout His ministry, such as rhetorical and directed questions. He asked questions that caused people to identify, connect, compare, contrast, classify, interpret, apply, and answer. In essence, Jesus used questioning to its fullest potential. Jesus uses questioning throughout Luke 6:20–49. In verses 32 and 33, He asks a question that causes His students to apply and think through the topic being discussed: "What thank have ye?" (KJV) Likewise, Jesus uses a question to begin His parable in verse 39: "Can the blind lead the blind?" This type of question not only causes one to think in physical terms (can the blind really lead the blind?), but it also creates an engaging entrance for His parable—it draws one in and makes one want to hear the end. Furthermore, Jesus uses questions to challenge His listeners towards action: "Can you see the beam in your own eye?" (see v. 41); and, "Why do you call Me 'Lord, Lord,' and not do the things which I say?" (v. 46) Jesus' questions are penetrating and compelling.

Humor

As mentioned earlier, Elton Trueblood, in his book, *The Humor of Christ*, argues that some of Christ's teachings are meant to be taken in the context of humorous declarations. Analogies such as the "camel through the eye of a needle" were meant not only to teach, but to teach humorously. In a similar fashion, Jesus uses humor amidst the serious topic of judging others in Luke 6:37–43. In verse 39, Jesus is in the middle of His discourse on judgment when He asks the question: "Can the blind lead the blind? Will they not both fall into the ditch?" This insert offers a humorous glimpse into the personality of Jesus. Of course the blind can't lead the blind, but Jesus' irony has a point: before you judge someone else, make sure your own life is clean. Jesus uses humor to declare truth.

On a personal note, I know that when humor is used in a lecture or speech, the influence on my life is greater. Jesus was able to utilize humor in an effective way to declare truth. Likewise, teachers should seek to use humor (tastefully) and foster an atmosphere in which learning can include a good laugh every now and then.

Object Lessons

When I understand something about an item a teacher is discussing, I am more apt to apply it and understand it in the context of its intended means. For example, if I understand what a wrench is, I can begin to assess (maybe with some teaching) how to use the wrench. However, if I do not know what a wrench is, I probably won't understand how to use it. In a similar fashion, Jesus used familiar objects to explain the truths of God's kingdom. He used seeds and fishing boats, among a host of other object lessons.

In Luke 6, Jesus used several object lessons to teach. In verse 43, Jesus used the idea of a tree and fruit. The people of the day were agriculturally based; they knew about the laws of the land. So, when Jesus made reference to a good tree bringing forth good fruit, they understood what He meant.

In verses 48 and 49, Jesus' analogy of rock and earth as a means of building a foundation would also resonate with His hearers. They understood that, in order to have a strong foundation, rock is superior to dirt. They understood that rain and the elements can destroy a dirt-based foundation, but a rock-based foundation is stable.

As in so many other areas, Jesus was the Master of object lessons.

Nurture: Ethics and Morals

Jesus' teaching methods went far beyond just technique. Jesus was not out to impress His students with slick methods. Jesus had something to say. He had truth to communicate and values and morals to proclaim. His educational objective was to make men better in Him. Alternatively, as C. S. Lewis stated, "Education without values, as useful as it is, seems rather to make man a more clever devil." Therefore, suffice it to say that any assessment of Jesus' teaching methods must take into consideration the "message." The ethical aspect of Jesus' teaching was the cornerstone of why He was teaching. Jesus was teaching the world of the kingdom and Himself—an eternally important message.

In Luke 6:20–49, the main emphasis in Jesus' teaching was on the ethics of the kingdom. According to R. C. Sproul, "Ethics [are] a normative science, searching for the principal foundations that prescribe obligations or 'oughtness.' It is concerned primarily with the imperative and with the philosophical premises on which imperatives are based" (Sproul 9–10). In short, Jesus was telling His students the truth about the "kingdom life"; what God deems to be ethical and right. It is with the "ethics" of the kingdom that Jesus fostered and nurtured a God-centered life. In Luke 6:20–49, Jesus uses several elements of human "nurturing": He corrects, clarifies, comforts, and commands. In essence, Jesus is encouraging and directing His students in several key ethical directions. He is utilizing, not only motivation and comfort, but also challenge and condemnation as tools to make plain His ethical teaching. Bluntly stated, He is teaching the truth and wants His students to understand what He is saying. Ethics are of utmost importance.

Corrects and Clarifies

Throughout this portion of Scripture, especially in verses 20–26, Jesus is found correcting improper ideas about the Law and living, as well as declaring the ethical mandate of the kingdom. And then in verse 27, He says, "But I say to you. ..." In effect, "It doesn't matter what you have been told by other teachers; this is the true proclamation." Jesus then talks about loving our enemies and clarifies the scriptural principles on judgment, among other things.

All teachers, from time to time, will need to utilize the dual relationship between correction and clarification. Teachers must correct misinformation and then clarify the information.

Comforts and Commands

In a similar fashion, Jesus' teaching on the ethics of the kingdom has the dual element of comforting and commanding. Jesus comforts His students by saying, "blessed," or happy are you when you live this way. Yet, Jesus doesn't stop here. He recognizes that comfort is a crucial element, but people also need commands and exhortation. Jesus does this in several ways. He commands them to "love," to "give," to "do good," and to "judge not," and so forth. In effect, Jesus is commanding them towards a new life, a new way of living. He is able to balance the scales between exhortation and edification in a wonderful way.

Likewise, all teachers need to comfort their students, to bring hope and call them "blessed"; yet, at the same time, teachers are called to command and direct them towards a higher standard: God's standard.

Conclusion

As the Master Teacher, Jesus is a model for us to look unto. We can study His "techniques" and "methods" and learn from His example. However, Jesus was not just a great teacher. He is God incarnate, and the ethics of what He taught have eternal significance, both for teachers and students. Therefore, teachers can seek the moral imperative from His example as well.

Saying that we model ourselves after Jesus is risky business. Jesus was and is perfect; He is the true *imago deo*, whereas humans are flawed and imperfect, and only reflect the *imago deo*. However, this is not to say that Christian teachers cannot look to Jesus and ask Him to make them more like Himself. We can! As Christian teachers, Jesus is to be our everything—Lord, King, Prophet, Priest, and example.

Luke 6:20–49 is a grand example of Jesus as a teacher. In a condensed fashion, it shows some of Jesus' methods and techniques. However, to get the fuller picture of Jesus as a teacher, one must look throughout the Gospels, gleaning the vast amount of wisdom that Jesus has to offer. True, this portion of Scripture shows the teaching environment, the techniques, and the nurture, but elsewhere one can find Jesus' heart in relation to His students and people, His thoughts on prayer and hypocrisy ... the list can go on. The bottom line is that in Jesus are the riches of the soul, and all who are thirsty, in need of direction and solace, can seek Him and find the peace and answers they need.

It is a privilege to search the riches from the world's greatest teacher!

PART II

THE FRAMEWORK

4

JESUS' FOCUSED SUMMARY: AN OVERVIEW OF EDUCATIONAL FRAMEWORK

"You shall love the LORD your God with all your heart, with all your soul, and with all your mind."

Matthew 22:37

The Greatest Commandment

Now that Jesus' learning and teaching style has been discussed, what exactly does this tell us as educators? Is there an approach that helps summarize His teaching style? What is the aim of Christian education as demonstrated by Christ? These are important questions. I believe there is a Christ-based approach towards education. This approach or summary is best translated in Jesus' summation of the law: "You shall love the LORD your God with all your **heart**, with all your **soul**, with all your **strength**, and with *all* your **mind**" (Lk 10:27, emphasis added). Here we see Jesus challenging and commanding His followers to relate to the Father and each other holistically. All the faculties of a person are to be pressed toward loving God.

Seen through the lens of education, Jesus' declaration is a call to educate a life; to mold and shape, not just the spirit, but the mind (academics), the soul (conscious thinking), and the body (the physical)—the entire person. Jesus' words also address how a student is to interact with others: "Love your neighbor as yourself" (Mt 22:39), which is the social (attitude towards others) element of Christian education. Therefore, it is safe to say that Jesus' summary of the law is very applicable to the education process, and therefore should be at the heart of the educator's aims and goals. First, we must look at the words of Christ.

When Jesus voiced the thoughts in Matthew 22, He had just been approached by a lawyer asking Him a question, "Master, which is the great commandment in the law?" Jesus' answer was, "Thou shalt love the Lord thy God with all thy heart, and with all thy soul, and with all thy mind ... And the second is like unto it, Thou shalt love thy neighbor as thyself" (vv. 36–37, 29 KJV).

Here Jesus summarized the Law and Prophets. Not only does this summary act as the foundation of Christian living, but as the praxis of Christian living. This summary can be used as a framework in all areas of Christian life: politics, education, work, and so forth. It is a monumental statement with far-reaching ramifications.

The Heart

The "heart" (Gk. *kardia*) is the "doing" aspect of the education process. Taken either literally or figuratively, the heart is the day-to-day reality of educating students. Heart-based education can be applied to many things: thoughts, reason, will, and so forth—elements that can affect a physical heart. Educationally, I relate it to the "doing" element of an educational framework. It is what keeps the body "pumping": teaching, homework, critical thinking, sports, cooperative learning, assemblies, and missions. Notice, the heart involves people. Not only is it the "doing," but it is the "story" of people; how the Lord has directed individuals throughout history. The heart element, in one sense, is the people's heart and story, but in another sense, it is

God's heart and story towards us. Therefore, this area educationally addresses community, story, doing, being, and relational qualities.

The Soul

The soul/spirit (Gk. *psuche*) is the immaterial (conscious: thoughts, ideas) part of a human. The soul is that which gives a person the ability to communicate with God through prayer and thought. Educationally, I relate this to the spiritual components of a person's life—the need for prayer, biblical meditation, worship, and Bible study. Throughout the ages, the fruit of the church has been the pursuit of goodness (right living), truth (the gospel and Christian worldview), and beauty (appreciating the creational magnitude of God). The "soul" element of the framework deals with aspects such as these. As Paul states in Philippians 4:8–9, "Whatever things are true, whatever things are honest, whatever things are just, whatever things are pure, whatever things are lovely, whatever things are of good report, if there is any virtue, and if there is anything praiseworthy—meditate on these things … and the God of peace will be with you." The soul is the aspect that is largely neglected in "secular" education, and therefore in the realm of the world. What a privilege that Christians have received the impartation of the Holy Spirit in the soul, that we might live unto God and pursue a life—the good life—in relation to Him. The development of the soul is crucial towards understanding a Christ-based framework for education.

Mind

The mind (Gk. *dianoia*) is understanding, intellect, and faculty of reasoning. Educationally, I relate this to the academic aspect of students—the need for academic challenges, critical thinking, accumulation of knowledge, and the understanding of wisdom. The Bible declares that the beginning of wisdom is to fear (have awe and reverence for) the Lord (Pr 9:10). A Christian's starting point in any area of knowledge is to begin with God—His person in Christ and His Word, the Bible. Our mind is to pursue His thoughts and be transformed by the renewing of our thoughts in relation to His purposes. Here a student needs to grapple with truth, worldview, logic, reasoning, cognitive inferences, and the base of knowledge known as "liberal education"—science, language, history, art, music, math, et cetera. The mind should be trained to reason and love Christ in the fullest possible means.

Equation

Though an equation is a presumptuous way of trying to summarize the educational pursuits of a Christian, simply because God does not fit easily into an "educational box," I include one here as a visual aid to demonstrate the balanced nature of what Jesus is calling His followers to do. Notice Jesus doesn't say, "Love God with your spirit only. And, by the way, the other parts as well." No, Jesus' exclamation is balanced—equality in the whole. Just as the Trinitarian nature of God is equal, so too should our nature equally be utilized in serving God: body, mind, and soul.

Think of educational pursuits as sitting on a seesaw, equally balanced, equally stressed:

Body   Soul   Mind

$$\triangle$$

Next, think of the three areas in terms of an equation so as to give a visual representation of the goal of Christian Education:

$$Body + Soul + Mind$$

Finally, add the summary of the equation: ministry to others.

$$(Body + Soul + Mind) + Service\ to\ Others =$$
$$Christian\ Life\ and\ Education$$

The integrated fashion of these areas speaks volumes. If we are to educate individuals well, then Christians are called to educate the whole child: body, mind, soul, equally and distinctively, with the outcome being that each individual learns to live the Christian life, and acts as salt and light in the world, serving others, and making disciples.

As already pointed out, Jesus' summation of the Law fits nicely with how He grew as a child (mentally, physically, spiritually, and physically). Another interesting parallel is to look at the relationship between Jesus' summation of the Law and His declaration as the "way, the truth, and the life." Though there is a not a clear delineation, one could draw a parallel as follows:

Heart	*Way*	"doing/ goodness/ people/ story/ community"
Mind	*Truth*	"objective reality"; truth
Soul	*Life*	"salvation/ living"; beauty

It is fascinating to observe how integrated Jesus was—on one hand, He was singularly focused, and on the other, He exemplified the full spectrum of human existence. Truly, His words and life are the "framework" upon which all Christians should base reality and education.

Paideia

Now that a Christ-based philosophy of Christian education has been established with the teachings of Jesus, it is essential that the rest of the New Testament support the principles described in the above discourse. You may be asking, "What does the rest of the New Testament have to say about educating?" Or, "What type of approach should be taken when educating?" Or, "How can one implement the framework given above in a specific way?" Or, "Does the rest of the Bible defend this view?" These are important questions. Though the larger arena of educational practice (scope and sequence, methodologies, and so on) will not be fully developed here, the general New Testament principle of educational application and formation will be established.

This is where the word *paideia* comes in. *Paideia* is a Greek word used in both biblical educational formats and secular (Greek-based) educational formats. Though the word was first used by the ancient Greeks, and Christians utilized it to communicate the full spectrum of responsibilities in child rearing. David Hicks summarizes one of the main differences between the Christian view and the ancient Greek view of *paidea* when he states, "Christian paideia ... urges man to aspire to be holy by loving above self the Creator and His creation" (Hicks 100). Simply stated, loving God and others. However, as shall be denoted, Scripture has an even broader view of the word *paideia*.

The word *paideia* is found in three sections of Scripture, and in a sense, is used as the disciple's prescriptive word for training; and more generally, a holistic term for education. Ephesians 6:4 translates *paideia* as nurturing and admonition. Hebrews 12:5–7 translates *paideia* as chastening. Second Timothy 3:16 translates *paideia* as instruction. As you read over the various definitions (nurture, instruction, chastening, and so forth), you are probably wondering how one word has so many different meanings. That is Greek for you! Actually, all three meanings are part of the definition of the word. In actuality, the original word had a far greater scope than just these three definitions. *Paideia*, as summarized by several New Testament writers, largely summarizes a Christ-based philosophy of education in that it takes into account the whole person. *Paideia* is the disciple's means of implementing the whole-person approach established and modeled by Jesus.

The Larger Context

The larger context of the word *paideia* is important in understanding a practical principle of how education is to be accomplished. For in understanding the biblical notion of how to educate, one is able to glimpse a little of how God views the education process.

According to A. T. Robertson, *paideia* is used for training and for the general education and culture of a child (Robertson 548. Vol. IV). We see from Robertson's definition, that the meaning of *paideia* has expanded beyond just teaching. It now involves culture. According to A. N. Vine, *paideia* means to correct by discipline and to train by action. It carries the meaning of positive training and the impartation of truth (Vine 97). With this definition, one can see the moral side of teaching: rearing up a child's mental, moral, and physical state. It speaks of a tutor concerned with the whole child.

Bullinger states that *paideia* means to train a child through discipline, instruction, admonition, reward, and punishment (Bullinger 146). With Bullinger's definition, the "discipline" side of education is stressed, setting a course of instruction for a student to follow, and helping the student to succeed in the course. Dr. Jaeger states that the Greek understanding of *paideia* is that of shaping a person in the context of the culture in which they live (Jaeger 314. Vol. III). In essence, it is the formation of a soul. With Jaeger's definition, a fuller approach is taken; it is almost saying the "training of a life."

The final definition seems to encapsulate the entirety of all the definitions. Christian education advocate Douglas Wilson states that *paideia* is an "all-encompassing enculturation of citizens in a culture. *Paideia* prepares for and ushers in a Christian culture [worldview]. *Paideia* extends well past the simple limits of an established curriculum; it describes an entire way of life" (Wilson 107). Here, the fullness of the word is seen; *paideia* is discussing a way of life, not just a set of curriculum and classes. On this note, Christian education is not just about the giving of facts (though this is important), but about shaping a life in Christ. It is the preparation of a child to think and act Christianly towards the world. *Paideia* is the New Testament way of stating Jesus' method of education.

Educational Motive and Process

Now that a Christ-based model has been established for the education process (Jesus as the center; a *paideia* framework; holistic education), the next question would be: "How do I go about implementing it?" As mentioned earlier, this dissertation is not meant to cover the complete scope of teaching strategies. However, it may be very helpful to suggest several concrete ways in which teachers, parents, and pastors can go about teaching children within a biblical framework.

To do this, certain questions need to be asked and their conclusions applied. In order to apply a biblical framework adequately, one must understand the conceptual foundations of why one is educating in the first place.

Motive

Before the brief "framework questions" are discussed, it is essential to determine why one educates. The motive is best summarized in Matthew 22:37 with the word *love*. Love is the foundation upon which all educational practicum takes place; it is the primary characteristic. Love is the backdrop, the essence, and the means by which education should take place. As Christians, we educate because we love one another and yearn for others to grow in the grace of God. We teach, challenge, correct, and discipline because we love those we are teaching.

To emphasize the "love" mandate in Matthew 22:37, one may read the passage as follows: *love* God with our heart; *love* God with our soul; *love* God with our mind. And *love* our neighbors as ourselves. Many like to concentrate on the mind, heart, and soul, but at times may inadvertently leave out the "love" element. As Christians involved in education, we cannot do this. Love is the focal point or the basis for which we are educating the mind, heart, and soul. Because God is love and He first loved us, we, as Christian educators, we must love, first and foremost, God, and then the students we are teaching. Students are not "numbers" or "bodies" filling desks; they are individuals created by God, to be loved and served.

Once the motive of "love" is understood, it is easier to implement the "framework" for education.

Process

After considering the motive, we now turn our attention to the process. The educational process can be seen as conceptual steps of development within a child. Education begins with the family (Dt 4–11; Eph 6:4), then moves towards those in the faith community

(Ro 10:14–15), and then the larger community. The overarching goal of Christian education is to prepare the child for living a life within the Christian context of Scripture. This includes looking at the student's person in relation to the wider community of faith. The community, then, acts as a steppingstone for influencing the world as light and salt. Parents, Christian teachers, pastors, and others are in the ministry of preparing students for a Christian life. Much like a citizen of the United States (or any country) is prepared for citizenship within its country, so too the Christian is being prepared for life within the kingdom of God.

One of the larger aims of Christian education is to provide a worldview upon which students are to view, weigh, and influence for better the society in which they live.

Many noted Christian thinkers have developed wonderful stages of the educational process. Dorothy Sayers, using the Trivium as a model, states that children should be educated, by and large, according to three stages: grammar (terms and usage of subjects), pert (logic), and rhetoric (communication and understanding). She fully develops her ideas in the essay, "The Lost Tools of Learning." Other Christian educators have stressed more developmental means of defining stages of growth. Most of these are fascinating theories; nonetheless, it must be stressed that they are little more than models for student development. The clearest declaration of Scripture regarding process and development would be that education begins in the home, then translates itself into the wider Christian community, and then lastly, when adequately prepared, to the world. This concept may aptly be called the Christian process of education: home, church/fellowship of believers, and world.

Building Blocks: Asking the Right Questions

Influencing the lives of individuals for the cause of Christ is one of the greatest privileges we have as a church. How we go about influencing people in a Christian context is dependent upon what God is calling the body of believers (the local church) to do: service, evangelism, expository teaching, fellowship, or a combination of these are all elements that the local church uses to reach a community. At the root of these endeavors is Christian education. As Christians, all we do, whether in church or out of church, is part of the educating process. We educate ourselves in the form of Bible studies, fellowship groups, and service as much as we educate the non-believer about what a Christian is, using the same elements. The core of the Christian faith is rooted in educating and teaching the world about Christ.

How we go about educating the world is a question that needs to be addressed by the church. As a church, we need to ask ourselves questions such as: What is Christian education? What is the message that we want to communicate? What curriculum should we use? Where should we educate? Who should be educated?

One of the more insightful books about developing a framework for Christian education is Karen Tye's, *Basics of Christian Education*, from which much of this section is drawn. Using Tye's "building blocks," I will attempt to ask and answer six basic questions: *What is Christian education* (concept)? *Why do we educate* (purpose)? *Where do we educate* (context)? *What do we need to know* (content)? *Whom do we educate* (participants)? *And how do we educate* (process and methods)? Additionally, I will discuss educational assessments and hindrances as seen by Tye. These final two areas are important in that they can help strengthen an educational program by assigning value to it and by assessing it in light of its strengths and weaknesses.

The intent here is to demonstrate that a framework of education does not start with curriculum, but the larger construct of how we implement a Christ-based philosophy in an educational manner. Tye's work is helpful in that it develops questions that address the topic in light of the larger principles established by Jesus. These questions and the dialogue that ensues will hopefully help give thought and direction to the larger foundation of previously discussed ideas concerning "the way, the truth, and the life," as well as the "body, mind, and soul" frameworks. The point that I want to stress is that in developing a framework, one must first discuss some crucial questions that will help assist in seeing the educational process come to fruition from a Christ-based perspective.

What is Christian Education?

The first question that needs to be addressed is: "What is Christian Education?" Tye expresses the importance of this question when she states, "I believe it is important because it will determine what we do in the name of Christian education. Our understanding of what it is will influence and shape what we do, why we do it, and how we go about this vital ministry of the Church" (Tye 9). Essentially, Tye is saying that answering this question is the first of the building blocks in the construction of an understanding of Christian education. It is the cornerstone of why we educate. It lays the conceptual foundation that is needed for all the other elements of the "building" blocks.

Christian education has been defined in several ways, all of which have unique aspects to add to the larger picture of what is Christian education. Many have defined Christian education as faith development, others as socialization and indoctrination, still others as conversion and nurture. When looking closely at the various ideas used to define the concept of Christian education, one can summarize these concepts into four main categories. Tye suggests the following:

Religious Instruction

This area specifically looks at the Christian faith. Education, here, is concerned with transferring the knowledge and practice of the church to people. It is here that people are taught the Bible, told the stories, and required to grapple with the theological ramifications of Christianity. Terms such as teaching, instruction, transmitting, conserving, indoctrination, belief formation, and the like belong here (Tye 10).

Socialization

The second area deals with how Christians interact with one another. It is, as some have called it, the "community of faith enculturation" (Tye 11). Socialization deals with how we as Christians participate and interact within our particular group: the songs we sing, the prayers we pray, the services we attend, the service we give, et cetera. Socialization is the "embodiment" of Christianity (Tye 11).

Personal Development

According to Tye, "personal development highlights the need for an environment that nurtures all persons in whatever stage they are in on their faith journey and helps them move from stage to stage" (Tye 11). The overriding characteristics of this element are "growth" and "development." The "personal development" stage addresses the issue of student growth and development, and patterns the educational environment accordingly. Personal development concentrates on the present stage of the student (young, old, et cetera), and determines the best way to meet the needs of the student according to the stage-related principles.

Process of Liberation

The final category is the process of liberation. According to Tye, this stage is seen as "a prophetic activity" (Tye 12). It is the stage at which Christians are called to participate in social action and develop themselves as light and salt in the world. Events such as mission trips, service groups, and ministry outreaches would be the educational model. The idea is on living and doing, not just on intellectual learning.

Tye ends with four areas of concern: religious instruction, socialization, personal development, and liberation. However, I feel she missed one important area—objective reality. Christians must seek out and define the world in which they live. The handiwork of God is manifest in the sciences, arts, and letters in ways that teach beyond just the social or personal levels. Objectivity delves into the realm of knowing epistemology, rationally based and substantiated by Scripture, and the God-given laws that govern our universe. Therefore, it behooves the Christian educator to teach not just religious instruction, socialization, personal development, and liberation, but objectivity as defined by science, art, and so on, and solidified by the Bible.

Broadening the Foundation

The final "conceptual" aspect related to the question: "What is Christian education?" is one of great importance. This area relates to "when" one should be educated. In the past, many people believed that Christian education was to be done in a classroom with a set curriculum, nice rows, and studious students, from the hours of 8:00 a.m. to 3:00 p.m. However, when looking at Scripture, one finds a different portrait painted. As an example, Deuteronomy 6:4–9 (KJV) states:

> *Hear, O Israel: The LORD our God is one LORD: And thou shalt love the LORD thy God with all thine heart, and with all thy soul, and with all thy might. And these words, which I command thee this day, shall be in thine heart: And thou shalt teach them diligently unto thy children, and shalt talk of them when thou sittest in thine house, and when thou walkest by the way, and when thou liest down, and when thou risest up. And thou shalt bind them for a sign upon thine hand, and they shall be as frontlets between thine eyes. And thou shalt write them upon the posts of thy house, and on thy gates.*

From this Scripture text, one gets the impression that education is to occur at all times and places, not just "at school." According to Tye, "At its heart Christian education is a communal activity done by the community of faith for the benefit of, and for service to, the world. … Education occurs in the context of the family … it is done in both formal and informal ways. Our Hebrew ancestors, as seen in Deuteronomy 6, had a broad view of education" (Tye 16–17).

Therefore, the view that education is to occur only in a classroom is not only misguided, it may be unbiblical. The Bible clearly teaches that education is to be a daily adventure between an individual and the community at large. People are to learn about the Lord in all areas of life, not just on Sundays or any other day. Every event and element that the church participates in should be one of teaching and instructing.

With this in mind, it is important that the church and school keep the truth of communal education in the forefront, not only for the student's sake, but for the teacher's and community's as well. When all understand that the church is in the business of educating its people and the world, more attention may be given to what it is doing in the areas of education, and the best means to accomplish its educational purposes in light of its call to disciple the nations.

Why Do We Educate?

The second question that needs to be answered is "Why do we educate?" This second building block deals with the "purpose" of educating. Understanding the "concept" and "purpose" are both essential to the overall "building" of Christian education. According to Tye, "Concept and purpose go hand in hand. We cannot fully engage in the various kinds of education ... unless we know the end toward which we are instructing. ... Our purpose shapes what it is we do as educators" (Tye 21).

How this "purpose" takes shape is dependent upon whom you ask. Daniel Aleshire believes that the purpose of Christian education is to "enable people to learn the Christian story, both ancient and present; to help people develop the skills they need to act out their faith; to help people reflect on the Christian story so that they can live aware of the truth of the story and how that truth is present in their own lives" (Tye 22). Thomas Groome suggests that the purpose of education is "to enable people to live as Christians, that is, to live lives of Christian faith" (Tye 22). Walter Brueggemann states that the purpose of education is to "ensure a continuity of vision, value, and perception so that the community sustains its self identity" (Tye 23).

By and large, these definitions have both internal (teaching the truth to the community) and external (teaching and ministering beyond the community) aspects. The various definitional "voices" call the church to evaluate the purpose of education in light of its concept. The purpose of asking "why" is to give substance and vision to the educational endeavors.

Using the principles established above in the Christ-based methodology, the question of why we educate becomes strikingly clear: we educate Christian people to love God fully and serve humankind as light and salt. Christians educate to train a life for service in the family of God. We educate because we are called to do so: lovingly, truthfully, and thoroughly.

Where Do We Educate?

The third "block" of the educational building deals with context. It asks the question, "Where do we educate?" According to Tye, context refers to the "settings, circumstances, and situations within which a particular event or happening occurs" (Tye 30). The noted educator Elliot Eisner makes a statement that causes one to see "context" not as a singular element, but a series of elements. Eisner states, "Schools provide not one curriculum to students, but three" (Tye 31). Eisner further defines these "contexts" as "explicit, implicit, and the "null curriculum" (Tye 31). The "explicit" curriculum is the actual content being taught; the books used and the material presented. The "implicit" curriculum is the surrounding atmosphere of the school—its building, schedule, relational qualities, and so on. The "null curriculum" is that what the school does not teach. According to Eisner, "The null curriculum includes areas left out (content, themes, points of view) and procedures left unused (the arts, play, critical analysis)" (Tye 31).

Based on Eisner's work, Tye likens "context" to awareness. Churches need to be aware of the wide variety of ways educational groups can approach teaching. Tye challenges churches and schools to broaden "our perspective when it comes to the settings and environments in which we educate" (Tye 37). How is a congregation to do this? Tye suggests three main insights on how to accomplish broadening the context of education:

First, understand that the "whole congregation teaches." To further this concept, Tye quotes from Maria Harris as to the various "forms" a congregation can participate in as a context for education. The forms are as follows: *koinonia* (fellowship), *leiturgia* (worship), *didache* (instruction), *kergyma* (proclamation), *diakonia* (service and missions). The bottom line is that every aspect of a congregation's life is a place for education.

Second, "There is more than meets the eye in a given context" (Tye 38). The main idea here is on the emotional, attitudinal, and cultural nature of context. It calls the church to recognize that safety, care, openness, hospitality, and cultural differences are all aspects that can be used to further the cause of education.

Third, "Context stretches beyond the doors of the church building" (Tye 41). The point made here is that there are plenty of educational opportunities that can be taken advantage of for teaching. The context does not have to be the church or school. As an example, the home and family are places where education should take place. The mission field and service projects are likewise wonderful "contexts" for learning. The final assessment is that Christian education does not have to take place within a church building; it can happen wherever there is a desire to teach and learn. The world is the classroom.

What Do We Need To Know?

The fourth question that needs to be asked when discussing the role of education is: "What do we need to know?" This building block addresses the area of "content." Content deals with the areas of "what we teach, study, and learn in the community of faith" (Tye 48). Content takes on many guises, and depending on the church or school, can take many forms. However, before one jumps to misleading conclusions about content, common "myths" need to be deflated.

According to Tye, the first myth is that "content has to do with facts and information." Though content does deal with facts, it does not exclusively deal with fact and information. The "fact" element of content is called cognitive knowledge. It deals with knowing about something. The problem with cognitive thinking as the only means of content is that it leaves out affective knowledge and behavioral knowledge. Affective knowledge deals with feelings, emotions, and attitudes. It takes into account the "soul" of a person. Behavioral knowledge calls the Christian to "do." Behavioral knowledge doesn't just know about Christianity, but lives Christianly. Deflating the myth of "cognitive fact only" shows that content needs to take into consideration the whole person: body, mind, and soul, not just the mind.

The second "myth" that needs to be addressed is what Tye calls "content as a set of curriculum resources" (Tye 49). The point made here is that content is not just a book or a manual. Though, like cognitive fact, books are important, they are not the summation of content. Once again, the whole person needs to be taken into account when dealing with content. Books tend to focus on the cognitive element of humans and leave out the other important aspects of human development. Tye states that "it is the entire course of the church's life that educates and we find content … throughout the life of the church" (Tye 50). Simply put, it is all the various elements of the Christian community that teach—from music, fellowship, and worship, to instruction and service. Education is not limited to just bookwork. Curriculum is the order of instruction, the totality of knowledge and experience, not just a set of books or prescribed lists.

The third "myth" is that "the Bible is the only real content that matters." Though, on the surface, this may not sound like a myth, the truth is that there are other subjects one can learn from other than the Bible. A case in point is an individual's testimony. Someone can learn from another person's "real experience" with the Lord, and benefit from the stories and heritage derived from their testimony, as well as from the Bible. In fact, much of the Bible is the telling of the stories of how God has touched, challenged, and condemned people. Since God is still in the "business" of changing lives, personal stories should be used as a means of teaching. Other areas are science or art.

The Bible, as the blueprint, gives the framework for the sciences, but it does not deal with them from a "textbook" standpoint; therefore, they are open areas for Christian inquiry.

The fourth "myth" is that "content is the concern of Christian education committees and church school teachers" (Tye 51). This myth is easy to see past in that it flows with all the other "myths." Education is to begin in the household of faith as a community endeavor, meaning everyone is to participate. One group of individuals should not, and simply cannot, educate in all areas. It requires the congregation.

So what does content include? What exactly does a congregation need to know? Tye gives several all-encompassing ideas. First, congregations need to study "issue-based" situations. Christians need to teach individuals how to think Christianly about the world; in essence, how to develop a Christian worldview. Churches should find contemporary situations in the world and discuss them from a biblical perspective. In this area, Harry Blamires suggests that the marks of a Christian mind should be its supernatural orientation, its awareness of evil, its conception of truth, its acceptance of authority, its concern for the person, and its sacramental "cast" (Blamires i). Other noted educators present the idea of creation, the fall, redemption, and sanctification as a framework.

Second, congregations should study "theological disciplines," what it is the church believes and teaches and how this belief affects the congregation and the world. Here, teaching involves not just "subjects," but the biblical integration of what these subjects say, or do not say, about God. Since God is the author of truth, all areas of inquiry and all subjects of academic knowledge are at the disposal of the Christian to either accept or reject. A good summary of the theological ramifications of integrated education can be found in Arthur Holmes' book, *The Idea of a Christian College*. In summary, Holmes states that there are four areas and concepts of focus: creation, human person, truth, and the cultural mandate.

The *Creation* area "imparts sanctity to all realms of nature and to human history and culture: (Holmes 15). The emphasis here, as taught by Holmes, is that Christians are not to have a polarized view of Creation. Instead, Christians are to "approach the works of God, probe their mysteries, and harness their potentialities with humility but with boldness as well" (Holmes 15). The point is that Christians should study and learn the language of the natural world and the humanities, since it is part of God's creation, and therefore open for inquiry.

The *Human Person*, as argued by Holmes, is "equipped by God with rational, moral, and artistic powers to invest for our Maker" (Holmes 15). He further states that the "educator's task is to inspire and equip individuals to think and act for themselves in the dignity of persons created in God's image" (Holmes 16). The task, therefore, for the Christian educator, is to value human life and the potentials it entails.

In relation to *truth*, Holmes' first principal states, "all truth is God's truth." Here Holmes is not stating that what people claim as truth is God's truth, but what is actually true, and therefore must be biblically verifiable. The second principal is that truth is unified, and Jesus is the center of the unity. The third point according to Holmes is that "Christian commitment does not restrict intellectual opportunity and endeavor, but rather it fires and inspires purposeful living" (Holmes 19). Therefore, we should help the human to grow and discover truth, both biblical and natural.

Next, Holmes deals with The *Cultural Mandate*. Here, Holmes argues that part of our responsibility in subduing the earth is to affect culture and to educate. He states, "to see every area of thought and life in relation to the wisdom and will of God and to replenish the earth with creativity of human art and science" (Holmes 21). In and through all this, is the task of educating about the world in which we live. Therefore, it is the Christian's responsibility, not only to pursue truth, but also to teach it in its fullest sense. Science, art, theology, and the like are all included on the table for an intellectual feast.

The third element addressed by Tye under the question: "What do we need to know?" is that a congregation should study the Bible: its stories, its heritage, its history, its theology. This may sound basic, and many may wonder, "Don't most churches do this?" The answer is no. Systematic, thorough, and expository teaching is needed in all facets of educational pursuits.

Fourth, the congregation needs to hear the ongoing "stories" of people's lives. Simply put, the educational process is to discuss all the elements of what the Lord is doing in people. It need not stop with theology and the Bible, but must include the contemporary and "living stories" of people's testimonies and lives. Returning to Holmes, when dealing with people, one must first recognize that a person is a reflective, thinking being. This being so, then, the first task of education, according to Holmes, is to "fan the spark and ignite our native inquisitiveness" (Holmes 30). Holmes sees that to accomplish the above task, one must have interdisciplinary approaches to learning, cultivate theoretical questions, formulate hypotheses, imagine new worlds for art to create, and examine the various worldviews. Second, a person is a valuing being. Holmes states that "values are more than feelings and they are not all relative ... the educational goal, therefore, is to teach values as well as facts" (Holmes 32). Third, a person is a responsible agent. Therefore, persons in educational areas need to be responsible in all of life's relationships as a stewardship of what God has created.

In either case, Holmes or Tye, the person's life needs to be addressed in an academic setting.

Whom Do We Educate?

The fifth building block of education asks the question: "Whom do we educate?" This area deals with the participants in the educational process. From the standpoint of simplicity, this area is the easiest to give a clear cut answer: the entire community of faith are those whom we educate, and consequently, the entire world through proclamation. At its heart, Christianity is a teaching faith. It tells a story; it communicates its truth; it calls for obedience.

However, in order to effectively educate the whole congregation, and in a sense, the world, three areas of understanding must be acknowledged. First, there must be an "understanding of the complex and multidimensional nature of human beings" (Tye 70). Christians must learn how people grow and develop so as to communicate the gospel in a clear way. Christians must understand that each individual has universal human qualities as well as culture-specific and individual-specific qualities. People are a combination of biological, theological, mental, and cultural factors; they are multi-dimensional, not one-dimensional. It is imperative that Christians understand to whom they are ministering, and not fall into the trap of feeding meat to a babe.

Second, Christians need to understand human development. Tye makes a good point in this area when she states that "it is important to see developmental theories as descriptive, as tools that help us to describe what might be happening in a particular person's life at a particular moment ... the problem comes when we try to use these theories in a prescriptive manner ... we tend to become judgmental" (Tye 76). The point is that there are many "theories" of how people develop, but the Christian should not get caught up in these "theories" as fact. Theories, by definition, cannot be infallible. That is why Tye's advice is good. Christian's should look into the theories, but understand them to be descriptive and not prescriptive. The theories can shed light on how humans develop, and in turn, help Christians in the task of educating both their people and the world. Therefore, the Christian should understand that people develop at different rates and that educational endeavors should be appropriate for the age group and readiness level of the students.

The third area Christians need to understand is how people learn. Having a basic understanding of the human brain—how humans perceive and process information—is very valuable. Once a teacher understands the variety of ways humans learn (kinesthetic, verbal, auditory, et cetera), using a variety of reflective and active teaching methods will not only make a learning environment bright and fascinating, but will help get the truth across in several different mediums.

Understanding how people learn is imperative and of great assistance when one is in the "business" of educating.

How Do We Educate?

The final building block question the church needs to ask is: "How do we educate?" This block deals with the process and method of educating. Tye is quick to point out that there is a difference between process and method. According to Tye, process refers to "the broad approach we use in educating ... a series of actions that we take in order to accomplish our purpose" (Tye 90); whereas method "refers to those specific activities and techniques that we use to carry out the process" (Tye 90). Both process and method are an intricate and essential part of the educational process.

The process of education should be broad, informed, and reflective. Process, states Tye, should "provide the blueprint for how we will go about our educational tasks" (Tye 93). So, how is the church to go about its educational tasks? Tye suggest that the process should include three main areas: experiential, reflective, and relational.

In the experiential stage, the learner needs to be engaged in all sensory areas. Geoffrey Caines states, "the learner needs to be engaged in talking, listening, reading, viewing, acting, and valuing" (Tye 94).

In the reflective stage, the learner is to be characterized by imagination, critical thinking, and "active processing" (Tye 95). According to Tye, reflection "calls for participation in a whole variety of questioning activities where we have the opportunity to ponder why we believe the way we do" (Tye 95).

In the relational stage, the learners should relate to one another as partners, companions, midwives, sponsors, and guides (Tye 97). These "images" give guidelines of how individuals can act in a community of faith. In their various forms, each of these words signifies a unique relational quality, i.e. midwife assists "giving birth to ideas and vocations; a companion is called to come alongside and 'feed' his brother in need; a sponsor is one who offers encouragement and makes accessible what is needed ..." (Tye 99). Tye stresses that "processes that are shaped by experience, reflection, and relationships will lead to learning and growth" (Tye 100).

The methods used in the educational framework are many. As mentioned earlier, Jesus, as the supreme example, used an amazing array of teaching methods: speech, cooperative learning groups, question and answer, dialogue, and so forth; the list could go on. However, the emphasis should not be placed on one specific "method" over another, but that a variety of methods or strategies are needed to fully communicate. Tye gives several key thoughts in relation to educational methods.

First, "Methods should be compatible with the content, the context, and the people in the educational setting" (Tye 100). Second, Tye states that "the broader your repertoire of methods, the better" (Tye 101). Third, "It is important to think through and practice a new method before using it" (Tye 102). Fourth, Christians must "remember that the purpose of a method is to help people learn" (Tye 102). These ideas are not the methods themselves, but rather principles to abide by when choosing a teaching method. The teacher needs to ask himself or herself whether a lecture or a skit would be more appropriate to teach a particular lesson. Another teacher may have to choose between role-play or cooperative learning groups. Whatever method is chosen, the teacher needs to have a clear vision of what is being taught. Methods are a means to communicate God's truth, not the ends in and of themselves.

Concluding Thoughts: Evaluation and Hindrances

One other question must be asked before we can conclude our building project. True, concept, purpose, context, content, participants, and the process and methods are all important foundational elements for a Christian education construct. But before we call our building finished, we must address the question: "How are we doing?" This question looks at assessment and evaluation. It seeks to determine whether or not a method is working. Tye defines assessment as the "means to measure something" (Tye 107). To measure something means that the group or individual must take "weight" of the learning process. Does it fulfill its intended purpose?

Evaluation

Evaluation, according to Tye, "means to ascertain or fix value and worth. It refers to the ways in which we judge and place value on something" (Tye 107). In all academic and educational endeavors, both assessment and evaluation are needed. Teachers and groups must ask themselves if what they did "measured" up to their expectations, and if it was "worth" doing. The answers and the conclusions may vary depending on whether or not the endeavor was successful. However, even if it was not successful, there is still an opportunity to learn from mistakes and make things better. In this way, the education process acts as an educator. It teaches us to become better teachers, students, and advisors.

Tye gives some practical principles for assessment and evaluation. First, do it in partnership (Tye 109). Work with other individuals who understand the purpose of your educational endeavors. Second, use a variety of approaches (Tye 110), such as surveys, questions, interviews, and so forth; assess the full program, using a variety of means. Third, get a lot of information to help assess the program (Tye 111). Do not just rely on one document to see if a program has been successful; get a wide variety of documentation to determine its value. Fourth, share the findings (Tye 112). It will do little good if you are the only person who knows the value of your findings. Share it with the church, the committees, and others who have a vested interest in the program. Fifth, keep the evaluation or assessment in perspective (Tye 112). According to Tye, "The purpose of assessing and evaluating is to help us see clearly" (Tye 113). Always know that it is not about personal failure or great success, but about working for a common educational goal for God's glory. It calls for our best, but at times may fall short.

The final bit of advice Tye gives is to establish a "plumb line."

A plumb line is the standard upon which you base your endeavors. For the Christian, this is simple. A Christian's plumb line is Christ and His Word. Period. However, within His Word, there are several options available: heart, soul, mind; justice, mercy, and grace, and so on. The point is to use Scripture to determine the standard.

Hindrances

The other area the church needs to be aware of is the hindrances that face an educational program. Tye points out several key terms that may become stumbling blocks for effective educational programs.

First is fear. Fear of failing. Fear of not knowing what to expect. Fear of not wanting to seek out other options. Tye states that "fear is the enemy of education. It causes us to draw back, to stop seeking, to stop wanting to know. It hinders our ability to be open, to look carefully and critically at alternative perspectives, and to explore new thinking ..." (Tye 120).

Second is false clarity. False clarity brings with it the notion that we have all the right answers. Its main danger is that it may stop some from continual learning.

Third are presumptions. According to Tye, "Presumptions are those preconceived notions, the taken-for-granted ideas that we have about people and things" (Tye 124). Presumptions are a problem, like fear and false clarity, in that they can cause one to stop learning and may hinder wanting a new look at things.

Fourth is routine. Routine is saying, "We have always done it this way." It doesn't cause a student to think outside the box, or to look at new alternatives or ideas. It keeps things in the status quo.

Fifth is what Tye calls the "tyranny of the urgent." This area is the need to have everything "now," in an instant. This is a hindrance in that not all things can be instantaneous. Not all events happen "now." Life has seasons, and seasons have to be waited for. The "now" mentality produces impatience and false expectations.

5

EDUCATIONAL CONSIDERATIONS AND CONCLUSIONS

Now that some "building blocks" have been stated and particular questions asked, thereby giving structure to a framework of education, it might be helpful to show the integration of the various elements that comprise a Christ-based philosophy of education. Here, my intention is to give some basic "considerations" about which the educator may think. I will not comment on them fully (for this discussion has amply done so), but only show, through a diagram, how they can relate to a Christ-based philosophy of education. In a sense, this chart is a conclusion of the various means and methods of a Christ-based philosophy of education. It builds upon prior charts and ideas. It is not meant to be all-inclusive; there are many more areas one could insert in the various boxes, thereby giving a fuller picture. But, hopefully, they will spark a correlation in your mind, seeing how the various facets relate.

Jesus' Person: the Foundation	Framework	Building Blocks— What is Christian education (concept)?	Points of Integration
Way	Stature ... Heart	Where do we educate (context)? Whom do we educate (participants)? How do we educate (process and methods)?	People-centered; telling a story, showing a way; social; sports; community building; methods and strategies; et cetera.
Truth	Wisdom ... Mind	What do we need to know (content)?	Academics; providential history; grammar; critical thinking; communication; worldview; et cetera.
Life	Spirit ... Soul	Why do we educate (purpose)?	Worship; inspiring the pursuit of truth, beauty, and goodness; meaning; koinonia.
Loving Others	Social ... Favor with man	Disciples and teaching.	Missions; service; evangelism; others-centered; action.

Column one contains the foundational (Christ-based) "philosophy" towards reality, as expressed by Jesus; it is the means by which a Christ-based philosophy of education must be weighed. In column two, the two framework models are positioned: Jesus' learning outcomes as a student and His teaching summarization as an adult. Column three has Tye's "building block" questions. Once again, these questions are included so that educators can think through the larger construct of educational practice, giving guidance as to the direction one must take. Column four contains the points of integration. This column, though not comprehensive, represents some of the ways the educational approach can be utilized in the real world; it is meant to give wheels to the car, so to speak.

In the course of this discussion, I have made an overt attempt at defining a Christ-based philosophy of education. In essence, I have taken the person of Jesus Christ, His declaration of deity, His life as a student and teacher, and His summation of the Law as the basis for an educational paradigm. Along the way, I have integrated Karen Tye's "building block" questions as a means to open up dialogue when developing educational practice and policy. I have overtly tried to steer away from curricular development and course content. Rather, my approach has been one of foundations and framework—defining a Christ-based philosophy of education that emphasizes the implementation of a Christian worldview and biblical model. Francis Schaeffer summarizes the point of Christian education when he states:

> "True Christian education is not a negative thing; it is not a matter of isolating the student from the full scope of knowledge. Isolating the student from large sections of human knowledge is not the basis of a Christian education. Rather it is giving him or her the framework or total truth, rooted in the Creator's existence and in the Bible's teaching, so that in each step of the formal learning process the student will understand what is true and what is false and why it is true or false. It is not isolating students from human knowledge. It is teaching them in a framework of the total biblical teaching, beginning with the tremendous central

thing, that in the beginning God created the heavens and the earth. It is teaching in this framework, so that on their own level, as they are introduced to all of human knowledge, they are not introduced in the midst of a vacuum, but they are taught each step along the way why what they are hearing is either true or false. That is true education. The student, then, is an educated person. ... A true education, a Christian education ... is giving the tools in the opening the doors to all human knowledge, in the Christian framework so they will know what is truth and what is untruth, so they can keep learning as long as they live, and they can enjoy, they can really enjoy, the whole wrestling through field after field of knowledge. That is what an educated person is" ("Francis Schaeffer on Education").

PART III
THE FRUIT

6

THE FRUIT BASKET

The final component needed in establishing a Christ-based educational foundation is what I call the fruit. This component deals with several important questions: What does the educational endeavor to look like? What books are useful? What curriculum is best? What is the end-product to look like? What are the educational fruits?

These questions are not easy to answer. There is not one set of books, one curriculum, or one picture of what education should look like. In short, the fruit of a Christ-based endeavor is varied. Some fruit may resemble bananas, oranges, kiwis, or mangos, Christ-based educational models may "look" different, but the essence must remain holistic, Christ-based, and biblical in order to accomplish the desired outcome.

The questions above generally deal with scope and sequence, the laying out of what is being taught and what books are to be used for each grade level and subject. As pointed out in an earlier section, Luke 2:52 gives a picture of what the student outcome should look like—growth in body, mind, and soul. In Christ-based education, the pervading question should not be about what approach or curriculum one is using (though this is important); the greater issue is producing educated Christians—individuals who have developed a Christian worldview that is consistent with Christ's teachings. The "nuts-and-bolts" of Christian education lie in seeking the mind of Christ for your student population.

Truth, Beauty, and Goodness

Historically speaking (specifically in the Middle Ages), the fruit of educational endeavors was to produce a love for truth (that is, God's truth), beauty, and goodness. The fruit of the educational process was to produce men and women who had a strong sense of what God deemed true, beautiful, and good.

Truth was defined as that which is objectively true; specifically that which was found within the Bible and nature. Men such as Aquinas taught that God's truth could be found in Scripture and in the natural world.

Beauty, in an ultimate sense, was that which reflected the beauty of God, His handiwork, and creation. It had a focus on the creational aspects of life: created beauty and creating beauty through the arts, literature, music, et cetera.

Goodness was the moral conscience of education. It was the yearning to teach ethics and biblical standards of living.

One could argue that the fruit of education is perfectly summarized in the words *truth, beauty,* and *goodness.* It is hard to deny that, at the hands of Christians, many true, good, and beautiful things have been created by those individuals open to God's working in their lives. One can think of a Bach cantata, Milton's and Donne's poems, C. S. Lewis' books, and simply thank God that they were open to His leading.

How did men like Bach, Donne, and Lewis arrive at such a point? Again, I do not think there is an easy answer. But I want to suggest a sampling of biblical principles that can be used as a guide in the pursuit of good fruit. These examples are not exhaustive. The challenge for every Christian educator is to let the Holy Spirit lead as you unearth principles in the riches of God's Word. For the purpose of this section, I will concentrate on four important scriptural precedents.

"Each tree is recognized by its own fruit."

—Luke 6:44 NIV

The first principle that needs to be established was spoken by Jesus when He said, "Each tree is recognized by its own fruit" (Lk 6:44). The greater context of this passage relates to the human condition—the fact that bad people produce bad fruit; and godly, or good people, produce good fruit (vv. 43–45). However, the application can relate to education as well. One can ask, when choosing books or curriculum: Is the curriculum going to produce godly fruit? Does the curriculum glorify God? Do the subjects allow for biblical application? Do the lessons call for the impartation of a Christian worldview?

Many times, it is difficult to judge the fruit before the curriculum is used, but there are some biblical passages that can be used as a grid for one to use in determining the biblical nature of the curriculum.

Finally, brethren, whatever things are true, whatever things are noble, whatever things are just, whatever things are pure, whatever things are lovely, whatever things are of good report, if there is any virtue and if there is anything praiseworthy—meditate on these things.

—Philippians 4:8

Philippians 4:8–9 is a tremendous help in determining curriculum. The first words we read in this passage are: "whatever things." This phrase testifies to the fact that the Christian field of inquiry is open. There are certain things in the world that are edifying and may not be directly revealed in Scripture. For example, the Bible does not act as a science textbook, but Christians can marvel at the beauty, grace, and sublime nature of the created order.

Philippians 4:8 presents us a gauge to construct curricular frameworks. The following presents a quick overview of the text.

Whatever is all-inclusive, but Paul defines it with several key words.

True is the reverse of falsehood.

Honest (noble) is that which is revered or venerable, dignified and worthy of honor.

Just are situations that are right between two persons.

Pure is to be chaste and free from stain or trouble.

Lovely is that which is pleasing to the senses.

Good report is that which is reputable, including the characteristics of kindness and respect.

Virtue is that which is honorable.

Praiseworthy has the notion of seeking out those things which ought to be praised.

Paul ends the passage with this command: "Meditate on these things." The idea conveyed here is that Christians are called think about these things, reason with them, and hold them in account.

Christians can use Paul's list when determining curriculum, books, novels, and materials for educational use. They are the paradigm upon which we can determine our educational scope and sequence.

> *Study to shew thyself approved unto God, a workman that needeth not to be ashamed, rightly dividing the word of truth.*
>
> —II Timothy 2:15 KJV

The next Scripture reference one can use to help guide the educational process is found in II Timothy 2:15: "Study to show thyself approved unto God." Notice two important words: *study* and *approved*. The Greek word for study is *spoudazo*. It has several meanings, including, "to make effort, to be prompt or earnest, to be diligent, and to endeavor to labor." The Greek word for approved is *dokimos*, which largely means "to be acceptable and tried."

Though the immediate context applies to Scripture, the principles derived from this text can be applied to the educational endeavor. We need to study, first and foremost, God's Word, and next, areas that concern Christians; namely, those things that fall within the Philippians 4:8 construct. Christians are called to "endeavor to labor," or stated simply to study hard.

Christian scholars are needed in all fields. The best way to become a "scholar" is to study; to be diligent and earnest in learning about a subject to the glory of God. A good rule of thumb is: study something, learn it, reason with it, and then communicate it; that is, talk about it and teach it so you can internalize it.

A Case: C. S. Lewis

A great example of someone who utilized his mental prowess for the cause of Christ is C. S. Lewis.

As a child, Lewis had hundreds of books at his disposal. Yet, having books is only one piece of the puzzle; the other piece is that his parents encouraged him to read the books. Additionally, his imagination was encouraged. He drew, wrote, created his "Boxen" characters, and wandered the countryside with his brother.

After the death of his mother, his father sent him to an English boarding school, which turned out to be a mistake as Lewis had a disagreeable time there. Later, his father sent him to a private tutor, the "Great Knock," Mr. Kirkpatrick. He taught Lewis logic and clear reasoning as well as Greek and Latin, pushing him to study, ask questions, and grapple with the material presented.

After a brief stint in the war, Lewis entered college. He studied hard, and majored in the classics. He graduated and later became an English Don. It was during his years as a professor that he met men such as J. R. R. Tolkien, and under their influence, became a Christian. From this point on, Lewis utilized his person for the Christian faith. One can only rejoice that the Lord used him to write popular theology, fantasy, science fiction, literary criticism, autobiography, Christian living, and more. His previous learning and hard work came to fruition in his Christian faith.

Several key elements from C. S. Lewis' life are important. The first is that he was encouraged in his academic life. His parents provided books, encouraged him to read them, and made sure he was tutored by exceptional teachers. Second, his imagination was encouraged. He drew, wrote, and explored. Third, logic and reasoning were taught. Fourth, language was taught and studied, which, in turn, helped with his reasoning and language development (writing, and so on). Fifth, he was encouraged to further his education (in his case, college), and he fine-tuned his earlier knowledge in a formal setting. Last, after becoming a Christian (he inadvertently surrounded himself with Christian friends), he utilized his prior study and hard work for the cause of Christ.

What we can learn from the life of C. S. Lewis is that reading good books, using one's imagination, having a strong teacher present, as well as studying logic, language, and determination are all very important characteristics for Christian educators to understand. But above them all is the resolve to study Scripture and apply its principles to every aspect of life, so that one can "study to shew thyself approved unto God."

> *And beginning at Moses and all the Prophets, He expounded to them in all Scriptures the things concerning Himself.*
>
> —Luke 24:27

History is vital! Much of the Bible is history, God's story. Suffice it to say that Christians should have a high view of history. In history, there is a beginning, middle, and there will be an end. Jesus, as shown in the above passage, teaches the importance of history; He began at the beginning (books of Moses) and walked people through history and Scripture to demonstrate that God had a purpose and plan for people—namely Himself. Other individuals in Scripture have used history (Moses, Dave, Stephen, and Paul, for example) to explain God's working in the world.

Teaching history chronologically allows the student to begin to understand the golden thread of salvation and their place in that thread, and allows them to learn lessons from the past.

Conclusions

As seen above, there are definite principles derived from Scripture that act as a basis for educational development. These examples, of course, are not comprehensive. There is a plethora of principles one can obtain from Scripture when assessing and developing curriculum.

The poet, T. S. Eliot, in his work, *Christianity and Culture*, gives several ideas concerning educational paradigms. First, he says educational systems "will be formed according to Christian presuppositions of what education—as distinct from mere instruction—is for" (Eliot 29). Second, he states, "Education will be directed by a Christian philosophy of life" (Eliot 30). Third, he says education "would contain both clergy and laity of superior intellectual and spiritual gift" (Eliot 33). Fourth, he states "Education must be something more than the acquisition of information, technical competence, or superficial culture" (Eliot 58).

All points stated by Eliot are important, but I draw your attention to Eliot's emphasis on philosophy (worldview). This is the gist of what curriculum should accomplish: the impartation of a biblical worldview concerning the nature of all things; developing a biblical philosophy of life that is true to, as Luther would say, the plain meaning of the text. Our job as Christian educators in developing curriculum is to let the Bible lead.

Overview of Curricular Distinctives

I. Defining Characteristics

    A. Begins with the father and family, moves to others, specifically the teacher—"in loco parentis" (Eph 6:4).

    B. Concerned with the whole child: body, mind, soul, and social interaction (Lk 2:52).

    C. Prepares the child for living a life within a Christian context with a defining Christian thought process and worldview as established by Scripture (2Ti 3:16).

    D. Full expression of the student's needs and interaction within a culture, including discipline, education, and social environment (Heb 12:5, 7).

II. Expression (Mt 22:37–40)

    A. Mind: Trivium-based (grammar, critical thinking, and communication) academic training; loving God with our mind.

    B. Body: servanthood, athletics, et cetera; loving God with our heart.

    C. Soul: spiritual training; biblical training; loving God with our spirit; strong emphasis on worship; emphasis on inspiring students with God's truth, beauty, and goodness; loving God with our soul.

    D. Social: peer interaction; missions; proclamation; service.

III. Biblical Curricular Distinctives

    A. History taught chronologically; shows God's providence (Dt 4–11).

    B. Introduction of foreign language in early grades; developing missions mindset (Mt 28:19).

    C. Grammar-based (grammar of core subjects), critical thinking-based (how to think clear and Christianly), and communication-based (how to verbalize and present ideas clearly).

    D. Primacy of worship (Jn 4:24).

    E. Service oriented (Gal 5:13; Mt 20:28).

    F. Integrated curriculum (understanding the totality of God's handiwork) (Pss 8 and 139).

    G. Questioning, listening, and a variety of teaching techniques as modeled by Jesus (Lk 2 and book of Lk).

CONCLUSION

Education is at a crossroads. For the Christian, there appear to be only two paths available. One path leads towards complete secularization of all academic and educational pursuits. This path is not concerned with biblical insight or Christian teaching, but in what "works" and what "counts" in the secular educational world in which we live. Teacher unions, college boards, and state-run educational institutions largely run this course. Ultimately, it is a path of failure and destruction, for it disregards the Lord.

The other path, a Bible-centric worldview, with Christ as the focus, is the only other available road. On this path, not only will the Christian student be encouraged in the things of the Lord, but will seek God's mind on what He desires, what "works" for Him, and what events "count" for eternity. This path is concerned with the whole child: body, mind, soul, and social interaction. It seeks to utilize a divine plan of educational focus, using Jesus as the role model and hero. This path may not be the popular one, and even may be considered antiquated, but God will honor those who honor Him.

The themes presented in this work (foundation, framework, and fruit) have offered clear direction for establishing and producing a Christ-based philosophy of education. Its aim has been to show that a truly biblical and Christ-based model is available and easily found in Scripture, and has attempted to point others to walk the path of Christ. Emphasis has been placed upon the parallel between how Jesus learned as a student to what He taught as an adult, fortified by His claims and teachings concerning Himself (which, according to John Stott, are supported by His character and resurrection as evidence of their truthfulness (Stott 5). A graphic summary follows:

117

		Jesus' claims:	Jesus the Student:	Jesus the Teacher:
Foundation	Biblical philosophy of education	"I am the way, the truth, and the life" John 14:6	He increased in wisdom, in stature, and in favor with God and men Luke 2:52	Love the LORD your God with all your heart, soul, mind, and strength Matthew 22:37
Framework	Jesus' Summary Heart, Soul, and Mind	Paideia Further New Testament Support	Building Blocks Asking the right questions	Hindrances to watch for
Fruit	Luke 6:43-45	Philippians 4:8–12	II Timothy 2:15	Luke 24:27

To further clarify the premises within this work, I have presented, as axioms, points that were either specifically dealt with or inferred. Hopefully, these points of reference will help you in praying through the development of a Christ-based philosophy of education.

Characteristics of Christ-based Education

- Christ-based education is derived from, and dependent upon the Bible as God's revealed Word. The Bible is authoritative.

- Christ-based education has as its philosophical base the claims of Christ, His declarations of who He is.

- Christ-based education is whole-child centered: body, mind, soul, and social components are of equal value.

- Christ-based education's greatest model of a master teacher is Jesus Christ.

- Christ-based education highly values varying teaching strategies. Jesus modeled a many different ways to communicate, from directed teaching to object lessons, from question and answer sessions to small groups. Jesus' strategies give Christian teachers the needed foundation upon which they can creatively expand to influence students and teach truth.

- Christ-based education finds a model of a strong classroom environment in Luke 2, thereby outlining principles for classroom success.

- Christ-based education values distinctive curricular approaches:
  - integrated curriculum: sees subjects as related and dependent upon one another
  - Early introduction of foreign language (mission-mindedness)
  - History taught chronologically

- Critical thinking emphasis

- Strong arts emphasis: fosters imagination and conceptual thinking

- Stresses communication skills at all levels: writing and speaking with grace and truth is paramount to clear thinking and the presentation of ideas

- Word-centric: values the written Word

- Christ-based education is dependent on the wider Christian community, local church, or pastor for teaching and learning. It is not dependent solely on a traditional day school.

- Christ-based education asks foundational questions when establishing a curriculum or a school: who, what when, were, and why.

- Christ-based education measures the fruit of its endeavors with Scripture.

- Christ-based education understands that love is the foundation upon which all education is done. Students are to be loved and formed, they are not just subjects sitting in a classroom.

- Christ-based education acknowledges the importance of worship in the educational realm.

- Christ-based education finds that good teaching is accomplished when the teacher loves, obeys, and serves God in front of his or her students.

- Christ-based education acknowledges that education begins in the home.

- Christ-based education should cultivate a love of learning across a wide vary of subjects.

- Christ-based education seeks to instill in its students the ability to know and understand a variety of subjects, reason with the material, study and contrast material scripturally, and prepare to answer the truthfulness or falsehood of all propositions.

- Christ-based education has both a cognitive level and a moral/ethical level; it calls us to know and to do.

- Christ-based education requires compassionate discipline for its students.

- Christ-based education is dependent upon the Holy Spirit to lead students to truth, and to foster a spiritual life within a student and classroom.

- Christ-based education points people to Christ, and is done for God's glory.

The above stated characteristics are a large order! I know it takes a lot of prayer, thought, and trust in the Lord to see them accomplished. One piece of advice I have in seeking a Christ-based philosophy of education is to focus in on three areas of emphasis: commitment, character, and community.

Commitment

Jesus calls His disciples to a life of commitment; commitment to Himself as Lord and Savior; commitment to one another as servants and friends; commitment to the world through service and proclamation; and commitment of ourselves as "living sacrifices." We as Christian educators must take seriously our commitment to Jesus Christ. It should be our hope that our educational endeavors will be a refuge for the committed; through prayer, Bible study, communion, fellowship, and learning, we seek to be a "company of the committed" for His glory.

Character

"The fruit of the Spirit is love, joy, peace, longsuffering, kindness, goodness, faithfulness, gentleness, self-control" (Gal 5:22). The fruit

of the Spirit is, in essence, moral virtue and character and character is the fruit of a Spirit-filled life. As educators, we must pray that our academic pursuits produce a life of fruit in our students and staff. The moral virtues we seek are the courage to acknowledge biblical authority, integrity, a commitment to justice and love in every area of life, conscientiousness of our tasks, helpfulness, servanthood, self-discipline, persistence, good family relations, active involvement in the church and community, and the call to be an agent of change in the world. In short, we must adhere to a high standard of character, signifying our relationship with Christ. In short, we must adhere to a high standard of character, signifying our relationship with Christ.

Community

The English poet and pastor, John Donne, wrote *"No man is an island, entire of itself; every man is a piece of the continent"* (Donne 445). As Christians, we are responsible to the Lord, to one another, and to our church. In essence, we are a living, breathing, and acting community of people designed for a relationship with the Lord and one another. Educators should seek to cultivate a community of caring individuals whose intellectual, social, and cultural life is influenced by biblical values so that the learning situation in life is, as a whole (heart, soul, and mind), approached from a Christian point of view. Christian Professor Arthur Holmes defines a community as "the social nature of those whose common stake in life and common values unite them in a common task." Furthermore, he states, "It is the sort of moral concern for others' well being that motivates hard and sacrificial work. ... Love, then, is not community-feeling but an inner moral attitude and commitment." (Holmes 80). Our learning communities should be characterized by love and deep relation with the Lord and service to one another.

It is my prayer that educational groups, whether day schools, home schools, or colleges, would seek the mind of Christ in all areas, and purposely develop a biblical and Christ-based philosophy of education. Yes, it takes commitment, steadfast character, and a community of like-minded believers, but it can and should be done for His glory and honor.

What a privilege it is to seek after Jesus, our great Prophet, Priest, King, Lord, Savior, and Friend! Life is an adventure with Him, and a life that is molded and fashioned after His is a thing to behold! Our primary function as educators is to shape our students after the example set by Jesus, who is the Way, the Truth, and the Life. May the Lord lead us as we follow Him.

APPENDIX A: EDUCATIONAL THEMES IN THE GOSPEL OF LUKE

Teaching and Learning the Jesus Way

This summary is directed to the Christian schoolteacher and the Christian disciple yearning to be more like Jesus. It is designed to summarize the pattern of Jesus as teacher revealed in the gospel of Luke; His variety of teaching strategies, methods, and means; but more importantly, how the Master Teacher not only taught the world, but changed the world forever. These observations are not meant as an exact commentary on the text, but are rather general deductions and applications.

- Luke 1 — Historical/chronological; shows flow and order
- Luke 2 — Stresses the importance of worship
- Luke 3 — Stresses the importance of preparation
- Luke 4 —Scriptures
    - Familiarity with text v. 17
    - Public reading v. 18
    - Compassion and good works vv. 31–43
    - Public preaching/speech vv. 42–44
- Luke 5 — Evangelism
    - Teaches through failure vv. 4–9
    - Evangelism vv. 27–51
    - Spiritual disciplines v. 36

- Luke 6— Sabbath — rest/break
  - Healing vv. 17-19
  - Went out v. 12
  - Blessing — public speaking — sermon vv. 20–49
- Luke 7 — Healing vv. 1–9
  - Uses Scriptures to demonstrate truth vv. 22–33
  - Interactive — use of stories and parables, asks questions, sets up scenarios vv. 36–50
  - Object lesson to point to greater truth
- Luke 8 — Parables
  - Stories
  - Explains meaning; we too need to explain meaning to our students
  - Questions — interrogative v. 30
  - Small groups — "inner circle" v. 50
- Luke 9 — Sends out to "do" hands-on "have students do what you teach"
  - Took outside to private time for— discipleship personal v. 10
  - Used an attention getter to start lesson v. 13
  - Orderly lesson v. 14
  - Question v. 18
  - Teaching on His life and death — what it means to follow Him — practical application vv. 21–26
  - Jesus had an inner circle v. 28 — took in as witness, intimate teaching
  - Rebuke and correction v. 41

- o Calls them to pay attention v. 44
- o Object lesson — "took child" v. 47
- o Use of analogy and metaphor v. 58 — to find deeper meaning
- o Challenge to students — "You go"
- Luke 10—Appointed — chose some to go out — teach lesson for us vv. 1–12
  - o Allows disciples to see intimate side v. 21
  - o Parables — vv. 25-37
  - o Call for devotions v. 37
- Luke 11 — Jesus was occupied — when interrupted, took opportunity to teach
  - o Analogy — vv. 5–8
  - o Explanation of analogy — clearly connected message with eternal truth vv. 9–13
  - o Perceives their thoughts, know where our students are v. 16
  - o Rebuke vv. 29–32
  - o Use of the daily to explain vv. 33–54 — lamp and dishes object lessons to correct and rebuke
- Luke 12 — Direct teaching
  - o Speaking from knowledge vv. 4–11
  - o Parables — to drive home the truth
  - o Direct teaching mixed with metaphors vv. 22–33
  - o Allows for questions during teaching v. 41
  - o Challenging teaching vv. 49–59
- Luke 13 — Jesus clarifies
  - o Parable vv. 6–9

- o "Teaching openly" v. 10
- o Parables vv. 18–21
- o Questions and answer — mixed with metaphor and analogy vv. 22–32
- Luke 14 — Question and Answer
  - o Teaching by asking a question vv. 3–5
  - o Parables vv. 7–14
  - o Direct teaching with analogy v. 34
- Luke 15 — Parables vv. 1–32
- Luke 16 — Use of analogy and stories vv. 19–31
- Luke 17 — Warns, reminds, and encourages concerning faith, thankfulness, and man's deceptions
  - o Direct teachings vv. 1–4
  - o Mixture of direct teachings and object lessons vv. 5–8
  - o Jesus answers critics
  - o Questioning minds v. 20
  - o Uses answer to speak deep truth to students v. 22
- Luke 18 — Truth revealed through lessons of irony
  - o Parables vv. 1–14
  - o Corrects wrong assessments vv. 15–16
  - o Answers questions vv. 18–23
  - o Direct teaching mixed with analogy, questions, and answers vv. 24–30
  - o "Took disciples aside/intimate teaching"; tutorial v. 31
  - o Asks questions to get answer v. 40

- Luke 19 — Clarifying the value of people and things
  - Personal, one-to-one teaching, called by name
  - Parable — to clarify a position
  - Sends students out to do something; responsibility v. 30
  - Anger and action is sometimes needed vv. 45–47
- Luke 20 — Maintaining strength of character when facing aggressive intimidators
  - Asks a question to answer a question; seeks to show the truth of the matter vv. 1–3
  - Parable; with interaction from people vv. 9–19
  - Parable to answer a question; uses object to clarify His position vv. 23–25
  - Answers questions vv. 33–38
  - Poses questions and answers them; directs to deeper truths vv. 41–44
- Luke 21 — Lessons of irony; warning to be alert
  - Sees an event and uses it to teach a lesson vv. 1–4
  - Question and answer vv. 7–28
  - Parable to help clarify His teaching vv. 29
  - Direct teaching "gives moral"; tells them what is important vv. 34–36
  - Public teaching/speaking v. 37
- Luke 22 — Lessons on provision, protection, and sacrifice
  - Prophetic
  - Intimate gathering; teaches about what will come; drew parallel between body and bread, wine and

blood; analogy, drew new conclusions based on old assumptions — "a New Covenant"

o   Caused them to think and question vv. 14–23

o   Teachers in the midst of disruption and debate; debate and argumentation vv. 24–30

o   Question and answer; question initiated by Jesus

o   Prayer with student (even though students failed, He still did it) v. 39

o   To a troubled student; still called him by name and caused him to re-think his position of doing wrong; notice He talked to him intimately vv. 47–52

o   Students will remember what teacher says even in troubled times vv. 54–62

o   Jesus gives straight, honest answers to questions vv. 66–71

- Luke 23 — Holds to truth despite suffering and persecution

  o   Direct answers, no explanation v. 3

  o   Even in times of distress, Jesus pointed students to greater truths

  o   Demonstrates grace vv. 32–43

- Luke 24 — Truth revealed through victory

  o   Students remember Jesus words vv. 6–8 Jesus drew near

  o   "Called" students, reasoned with students, asked questions — teacher

  o   "Sets up a scenario" with question vv. 13–18

  o   Intimate gathering

  o   Expounded — exegetical in-depth teaching vv. 25–27

- o Based on teaching, students were intensely impacted by the truth of His words v. 32
- o Students began to share what they had learned with others v. 34
- o Stood in the middle, not just in front v. 36
- o Asks questions to calm and challenge them vv. 36–43
- o "Opened" their understanding v. 45
- o Helped them "comprehend" v. 45
- o He blessed them v. 50
- o Corporate worship v. 52

APPENDIX B: GOD THE FATHER

One of the dangers of presenting an Christological philosophy of education is that the other two persons of the Godhead seem to take a back seat. This is not my intention, for I firmly believe that in Christ is God's will for the educational process. However, for the sake of clarity, the next two sections will give a glimpse of the other two persons of the Godhead, thereby allowing for a distinctly Trinitarian view of education.

Attributes

One of the clearest ways to assess the vastness of God the Father is to look at His attributes. Attributes are the descriptive terms used when looking at the character of God. It is through God's character that a picture of His heart and purpose is seen in relation to man and reality. One of the foundational facts about the Father is His creative and sovereign character. It is He that, with the Son and Spirit (Ge 1), created the universe and all therein. It is in Him and through the Godhead that physical reality continues to be stable, life conveys meaning, and history is providentially directed.

Educationally, this allows Christians to employ their mental, spiritual, and bodily faculties in all areas of inquiry. The universe belongs to the Lord, and we as His children are able to study it, analyze it, and seek His mind in relation to all things. The Father is the substance and source of all that is; therefore, the privilege of studying His handiwork in creation, moral law, et cetera, is an ongoing adventure, unraveling mysteries for Christians to pursue and investigate.

God's Word

To learn about God, one must begin with the Bible. It is in the Bible that we find God's revelation of Himself. God is the same in both the Old and New Testaments. The Hebrew and Greek names of God in the Old and New Testaments are intimately related to His nature and attributes. His names, attributes, and character are forever unchanging, and the Bible is the source of disclosure of His fixed character and person. One finds in both the Old and New Testaments "pictures" of God's nature. Though one must always understand that God's ways are forever beyond ours, it is still fitting to look into His revelation of Himself to learn from and apply the truths accordingly; for in the character of God, Christian educators can see the heart of God in relation to students and all people.

The Father is *immutable*. God is unchangeable. His nature remains the same throughout all existence. Taken from an educational standpoint, this is good news. What we teach students about God and the created universe is true, for this age, and all ages. God's character, will, and person is perfect and trustworthy in all areas and fields of inquiry. How God reveals Himself in the Bible, nature, history, and so forth, will be steadfast and unmovable.

God is *eternal*. God never had a beginning and will never have an end. Educationally, this attribute relates to immutability. God's eternal state and His unchangeable nature suggest that God's providential view of reality (history, science, et cetera) is perfect, and therefore open for investigation, study, and academic focus.

God is *immaterial*. God's person is not wrapped up in the physical nature; He is Spirit. Just because God is Spirit does not mean that Christian educators should not study the physical realm. On the contrary, we should, for the physical realm is God's handiwork—His creative act. God's immaterial nature also suggests that the physical world is not an end in and of itself. There is more than just the physical. The Christian position is not a materialist position. Because there is a spiritual world, Christian educators must teach about the spiritual realm: God, angels, Satan, and so forth.

Likewise, Christians must teach about the spiritual nature of man, which involves: his soul, his need for salvation, ethics, the fruit of the Spirit, et cetera.

The Father is *immense*. God's immensity literally means "not measurable." God is not limited to space or time; He is present everywhere and at all times. He is transcendent or omnipresent. This attribute of God is an exciting one for educators, for in it one finds that there is no end to understanding God's handiwork. Our educational pursuits here on earth will be ones of constant inquiry into space, time, and knowledge; we will never "figure" out God or the entirety of His ways. Once we learn something new or discover a new law, there will always be something original we have yet to discover about the immensity of God and the world He created.

The Father is *all-powerful*; He is *omnipotent*. God's omnipotence is an important doctrine in helping us understand that God can transcend the created order. He is powerful to do so. He can invade space with miracles; He can invade time with Himself—Christ; He can change the flow of history, laws, and nature; because of His power, the supernatural element of His person comes into the light. It is because of His power that we can accept the naturally unexplainable events in life, and trust that they can, and do, occur.

The Father is *omniscient*. He knows everything of the past, present, and future; there is nothing He cannot, or does not know. There is nothing I as a human can teach Him. For an educator, this is great news! For when I abide in God, I know I am abiding in an unfailing reality. When I teach His ways, I am resting in truth and complete knowledge. There is nothing I can think, say, or do that may surprise Him. In an ultimate sense, He is to be the very definition of a Christian existence; the living reality of who we are.

God is *wise* (*chakam*). He knows not only all things, but He knows the right course to take, one that is profitable and good. Much in the Bible is God's wisdom—the teaching of the "good life." As educators, we should always be seeking God's wisdom. We should search it out in Scripture, seek it in prayer, and teach it to our students.

In Him are found the wise words, actions, and sources of what is good, true, and beautiful.

God is *ineffable*. He is majestic and beautiful. He is worthy of praise, honor, and exaltation. This area is key for educators to understand and implement. We need to cultivate an atmosphere of worship—in song, words, actions, and more generally, in all of life. Humans are created to worship God, and in worshiping Him, not only does it give us purpose, meaning, and pleasure, but it also cultivates an element that secular education does not give—the life of the Spirit. In worshiping God, we begin to understand His worthiness, His beauty, and His love for all creation; and in turn, He blesses His children and opens up a sea of grace, mercy, and love. He gives us Himself.

God is *righteous* and *holy*. He is set apart from the created order; He is perfect. Understanding God's righteousness is pivotal. For in doing so, we begin to see that God is perfectly good and we are not. The understanding of His holiness and our sinfulness becomes clear. Even more so, God's holiness shows us that we need a Savior, one who will deliver us from our sin. God's holiness is an important facet to teach. As educators, the recognition of God's perfection and righteousness should be taught, not only as truth, but as a means to understand the sinful nature of humanity. The topic of righteousness is a good integration point for discussing issues of right and wrong—why something is deemed wrong, and why something is deemed right. It also acts as a springboard to discuss the larger cultural issues of meaning, law, art, music, and so on. It also is a good topic of discussion in relation to God's judgment of sin and unrighteousness.

God is *love*. His character is omni-benevolent; that is all-loving and all-good. His affection toward His creation and children is one of goodwill and tenderness; He is full of mercy and compassion. For Christian educators, love is to be the reigning characteristic. Love is to be the fruit of all fruits. It should determine our disposition as well as our actions. Love for God, family, and students is a necessity for

Christian educators. Love is the universe upon which the stars and galaxies move. Love is the hidden unifying answer for all relations, actions, and yearning.

APPENDIX C: GOD THE SPIRIT

This section proposes to draw a parallel between the work and person of the Holy Spirit to the task of educating people, specifically within a Christian education realm. Though, on the surface, it appears that the two topics may be interdependent from one another; yet, upon further examination, one finds fascinating similarities. Take for instance the role of illumination. The Holy Spirit does illuminate the heart and mind of Christians, pointing them to Christ and ultimate truth. Likewise, Christian education, through the Christian teacher, should set out to do the same: namely, illuminate the mind with the truth of God and set the heart aflame of the students being taught, and more specifically, point students to Christ.

Another fascinating similarity is that of the topic of truth. The Holy Spirit teaches truth, and as part of the Godhead, is truth. This type of truth is sometimes called revealed truth. Likewise, the role of the educator is to do the same: teach truth, or at least a byproduct of truth, a practical application of governing truth (Physics or Math as an example). This type of truth is at times called general truth. Obviously, there are some differences here in relation to truth. The Holy Spirit is infallible, and as the third person of the Godhead, communicates ultimate and perfect truth. People, on the other hand, aren't infallible, so our perception may not truly be "true"; yet, the task of the educator is nonetheless appropriate: to teach truth in accordance with verifiable fact; and more specifically, for the Christian educator, truth that is biblically true.

In order to further demonstrate similarity between the two topics and show how the task of education is similar to that of the person and work of the Holy Spirit, several areas must be discussed.

First, this section will briefly look at the person and work of the Holy Spirit, with a special emphasis placed on two of His work attributes: teaching and knowledge. Second, it will discuss the gift of teaching. Third, it will look at the role of Christian education and what it is that it should accomplish in the classroom and the student's life. Lastly, it will summarize how Christian education is to model, and more importantly, rely on the person of the Holy Spirit to accomplish its goals and means.

Characteristics

Can a stone bring life? Can a desk ensure spiritual health? Can something other than a personal, divine being promise growth and fruitfulness (and supply it)? Can asphalt teach truth? The answer to all the above questions is "No." Only a personal, living, supernatural being can promise life, health, eternal life, and other such weighty, philosophical matters. In short, only God is sufficient for such claims. The Holy Spirit, as the third person in the Godhead, perfectly exemplifies qualities such as the aforementioned. The Holy Spirit teaches truth, brings comfort, convicts, is grieved, and has a host of personal and divine qualities. Simply put, the Holy Spirit is God and does relate to the world in a personal, intimate fashion. In order to understand how education relates to the Holy Spirit, one must understand the person and work of the Holy Spirit. In order to understand the attributes of the third person of the Godhead, and how these attributes shape the teaching process, we must first look into the details of who and what the Holy Spirit accomplishes in the world.

The Personality of the Holy Spirit

The personality of something is that which possesses the attributes, properties, and qualities of personhood such as will, emotion, and intelligence. The Holy Spirit accomplishes all of these. The Bible tells us that the Holy Spirit is a comforter (Jn 14:16). Therefore, He is able to comfort and bring solace as a person. The Holy Spirit can be lied to (Ac 5:3), resisted (Ac 7:51); blasphemed (Mk 3:28). Therefore, we can conclude the Bible sees the Holy Spirit as a being, One that has relational qualities. Furthermore, the Holy Spirit can act as a person. He can speak (Ac 13:2), intercede (Ro 8:26), teach (Jn 14:26), commune (2Co 13:14), strive (Ge 6:3), and guide (Ac 16:6). Finally, personal pronouns, such as He (Jn 14:26), are used to identify the Holy Spirit, inferring personality. The Bible is clear in its declaration that the Holy Spirit is indeed a person.

Attributes of Deity

Likewise, the Holy Spirit exudes divine qualities. He is eternal (Heb 9:14), omnipresent (Ps 139:7–10), omniscient (1Co 2:10), and omnipotent (Lk 1:35). Additionally, there are divine references given to the Holy Spirit (2Co 3:18) and divine works attributed to the Holy Spirit (Ge 1:1 and Ps 33:6). It is fair to conclude, like personality, that the Bible is clear that the Holy Spirit is divine.

Works of the Holy Spirit

Jesus tells us in John 16:8 that the Holy Spirit will come and "convict the world of sin, and of righteousness, and of judgment." Therefore, we can conclude that the primary responsibility of the Holy Spirit is to impress upon people the fact that they are sinners in need of a Savior, and then point them to Christ, testifying of His redemptive nature. Yet, the work of the Holy Spirit does not end here. The Holy Spirit also regenerates the believer (Jn 3:5), indwells the believer (1Co 6:19), seals the believer (Eph 1:13), fills the believer (Ac 2:4), empowers the believer (Ro 8:2), guides the believer (Gal 5:18), and anoints the believer (1Jn 2:27). In short, the Holy Spirit is the active agent in the life of the believer in whom the Christian has the most contact within this age.

However, the work of the Holy Spirit doesn't end here, either. The Holy Spirit has had a place in history creating (Ge 1), bestowing artistic gifts (Ex 28:3), generating leadership (Nu 27:18), providing wise kingly rule (Isa 11:2), and most importantly, had a defining and intimate relation with Jesus Christ, whereby Jesus was conceived, led, anointed, crucified, and raised in the power of the Spirit.

Names of the Holy Spirit

Names for the Holy Spirit can also give the believer a glimpse into the role that the Holy Spirit has played and is currently fulfilling. Take for instance the name *The Holy Spirit*. *The* (one and only definite article), *Holy* (set apart and sanctified), and *Spirit* (immaterial and immanent), which itself gives a lot of information about who the Holy Spirit is. Other names include the Spirit of grace (Heb 10:29), the Spirit of burning (Mt 3:11), the Spirit of promise (Eph 1:13), the Spirit of glory (1Pe 4:14), and the Spirit of God (1Co 3:16). Additionally, the Holy Spirit is likened to a dove (Mt 3:16), fire (Ac 2:3–4), oil (Lk 4:18), a seal (Eph 1:13), water (Jn 4:14), and wind (Jn 3:8). As one can see, Scripture is replete with penetrating insight into the person and work of the Holy Spirit. However, there are two names that specifically relate to the topic at hand (drawing similarity between education and the Holy Spirit): the Spirit of truth (Jn 14:17; 15:26; 16:13; 1Jn 5:6) and the Spirit of wisdom and knowledge (Isa 11:2; 61:1).

The Spirit of Truth

As God is to love, so the Holy Spirit is to truth. Jesus stated that "I will pray the Father, and He will give you another Helper, that He may abide with you forever, even the Spirit of truth" (Jn 14:17); and further, "But when the Helper comes, whom I shall send to you from the Father, the Spirit of truth who proceeds from the Father, He will testify of Me (Jn 15:26); and finally, "When He, the Spirit of truth, has come, He will guide you into all truth; for He will not speak on His own authority, but whatever He hears He will speak" (Jn 16:13). As spoken by Jesus, the Holy Spirit is to lead, counsel, confer, and testify in and to the truth. In a logic/logos sense, Christ is truth incarnate; He is the purveyor of reality, and the Holy Spirit is the messenger and revealer of this truth. In an ultimate sense, the Holy Spirit is the communicator (and objectively "the being") of all meaning and substance; He is the resonating foundation of all fact, physical law, and objective reality. Truth, as stated here, concerns itself with all existence, be it a belief, thought, statement, or representation that corresponds to reality as it truly is. As Dr Carl Henry states, "Truth is truth because God thinks and wills it; in other words, truth depends on the sovereignty of God" (334). Furthermore, all truth is dependent upon what God has revealed in Scripture and the natural world. Again, Dr. Henry, "Since God is the source and ground of all truth, all truth is in some sense dependent upon divine disclosure ... truth consist of cognitively meaningful propositions; the totality of these propositions constitutes the mind of God" (Henry 336). In essence, the Holy Spirit is communicating the mind, emotion, and heart of God. God eternal (Father, Son, and Holy Spirit) is the cause of all mental, moral, and spiritual illumination upon which the Holy Spirit communicates and reveals truth to the world.

For the Christian educator, the pursuit of truth should be forefront in all he or she does. Christians are to think the thoughts of God, or at least, pursue to the highest degree to think the thoughts of God. These thoughts should encompass all academic, spiritual, and moral areas of investigation. Whether one is teaching Bible or Geometry, the need for objective truth is of great importance. How is one to teach a course or topic truthfully? For the Christian, the answer is by the Holy Spirit, through the inspired Scriptures. Scripture, as inspired by the Holy Spirit, is the guidebook "worldview" by which we interpret life and existence. It is through the Bible that we grasp the mind of God. I agree with Dr. Henry Morris when he states, "there is no boundary or dichotomy between spiritual truth and secular truth; all things were created by God and are being sustained by Him. Therefore, we can learn any aspect of truth only in accordance with His will to reveal it" (Morris 29). Dr. Jay Adams states a similar decree when he says, "Christian education depends on the Spirit's illumination and application of His Book, the Bible, for the correct perception and relationship of every fact, and on His energizing power for living according to biblical truth in all aspects of life" (Adams 87). The Holy Spirit inspires and conveys the truth, Scripture is the written truth, and the

Christian teacher is to faithfully teach and uphold the truth, in any academic or objective field of inquiry.

The Spirit of Wisdom and Knowledge

The picture painted by Isaiah the prophet, in chapter 11, portrays the Holy Spirit as wisdom and knowledge. The Hebrew word for wisdom in this verse is *chokmah*. It has several meanings: knowledge, experience, intelligence, insight, and judgment among them. It encapsulates the whole range of intellectual and experiential states of being. The Hebrew word for knowledge is *biynah*. Among its various meanings are "insight, prudence, and intelligence." Knowledge has three main "types," all of which can proceed from the Holy Spirit, and are accessible to man; and one, that I call divine knowledge, which directly corresponds to God, to which man does not have access. The important point being made here is that the Holy Spirit has complete knowledge, from temporal situational knowledge to divine knowledge. His knowledge is thorough and complete.

The first area of knowledge is *Knowledge by Acquaintance*. This type of knowledge relates to something directly involving one's consciousness. Such as, I know this book is in front of me. It is a direct awareness of the actuality of the object. With this type of knowledge, the Holy Spirit knows what truly is objectively real. He knows what was created and how the created order is sustained. Therefore, His understanding is complete in the associational realm; He is acquainted with all things that are objectively real.

The second type of knowledge is what Dr. J. P. Moreland calls *Know-How Knowledge*. This is best understood in terms of knowing how to do something: I know how to read. I know how to write. It involves prescribed behavior and the ability to accomplish the act of what one is claiming to know how to do. Again, here the Holy Spirit inherently "knows" all behavioral patterns and ambitions of knowing, thus fulfilling this area of knowledge. His knowledge of the insights and acts of the will are, once again, complete and thorough.

The third type of knowledge is called *Knowledge by Description*. This type of knowledge is also called propositional knowledge. It has more philosophical overtones, dealing with content and statements. An example of this would be the statement, "I know that George Bush is the president." Again, whether the statement is correct or not (as proposed by the person), the Holy Spirit is acutely aware of its truthfulness; He knows the heart and motive of the person and is therefore cognitively knowledgeable of the proposition and inherently maintains the objective reality of such a statement.

The fourth type of knowledge is *Divine Knowledge*. This type of knowledge only relates to God. Man can neither comprehend nor grasp the complexity of it, nor do I believe he ever will. It is the cohesive glue to which wisdom and knowledge are bound. The psalmist declares, "Such knowledge is too wonderful for me; it is high, I cannot attain it" (Ps 139:6). This type of knowledge is the icing on the knowledge cake; it is what makes God, God. Simply put, it is the knowledge that knows everything. It is directly related to the omniscience of God.

Wisdom and knowledge, like truth, are uniquely qualified in that both God and humankind can produce them. However, like truth, God (and in this case specifically, the Holy Spirit) is their ultimate source and infallible author. Only God infallibly denotes and communicates true wisdom and knowledge. God inherently possesses all truth, and therefore, in knowing all truth, He exhaustively knows all objects of knowledge and wisdom. Unlike God, man's knowledge and wisdom is limited. He is only capable of ascertaining objective realities by what has been revealed by God. However, this being the case, man is still called to pursue knowledge and wisdom. We know that the beginning of wisdom is to have reverence, awe, and fear of the Lord (Pr 9:10). So any starting point in attaining wisdom and knowledge is through God and His Word as inspired by the Holy Spirit.

According to Dr. Carl Henry, God's knowledge is "more than comprehensive; it is also eternal (Acts 15:18). ... Only God has perfect knowledge ... and divine knowledge is timeless and rules our temporal succession" (Henry 269–270). Simply put, pure and objective divine truth, knowledge, and wisdom are from God, all untruth and error are not.

As Christian educators, the task at hand is to prescribe God's wisdom and knowledge to the objective reality of the world as it is. Educators must present a Christian worldview, a framework upon which the world is understood. Here again, the Scriptures, as inspired by the Holy Spirit, are the key. The Bible is the framework upon which all knowledge, wisdom, and understanding rest. It is God's letter (if you'll excuse the simple analogy) to humankind. In it, one can find the unfolding drama of creation, the fall, redemption, the church, and Christ's return. And by the integrity of Scripture, one can begin to ascertain the hidden, or unwritten, elements of life. We can find the principle of all physical, moral, and spiritual existence. We can be inspired to seek the fruit of God's laws in the natural realm, to uncover the majestic work of His brilliant mind, and to replicate the wondrous beauty of His artistic hand. As Dr. Morris states, "Scripture, taken in context, and properly applied … provides the basic framework and guiding principles within which all truth, wherever found, must be interpreted and utilized" (Morris 28).

It is by the inspiration of the Holy Spirit in Scripture, the natural realm, and in the hearts of man, that the actualization of wisdom and knowledge comes to fruition. It is when a Christian teacher seeks the guidance of the Holy Spirit in prayer and in the Bible, that wisdom, truth, and knowledge becomes manifest in the totality of life and thought. It is when the unifying principle of "Christ is the truth" and the "Holy Spirit communicates the truth," that a comprehensive foundation of truth and knowledge can exist, which demonstrates an important facet of the Holy Spirit's attributes.

WORKS CITED

Adams, Jay E. (1982). *Back to the Blackboard*. Presbyterian and Reformed Publishing Company. Phillipsburg, New Jersey.

Anthony, Michael J., and Warren S. Benson (2003). *Exploring the History and Philosophy of Christian Education: Principles for the 21ˢᵗ Century*. Kregel Publications, Grand Rapids, Michigan.

Barclay, Robert. (1975). *The Gospel of Luke*. Westminster Press. Philadelphia, Pennsylvania.

Barnes, Albert. (2002). *Albert Barnes Notes on the* Bible. E-Sword Bible Software. www.e-sword.net.

Blamires, Harry (1963). *The Christian Mind* (CM). Servant Publication. Ann Arbor, Michigan.

Bloesch, Donald. (1978). *Essentials of Evangelical Theology: Volumes 1 & 2*. Prince Press. Peabody, Massachusetts.

Bruce, Gustav Marius (1928). *Luther as an Educator*. Wipf and Stock Publishers. Eugene, Oregon.

Brueggemann, Walter (1982). *The Creative Word*. Fortress Press. Philadelphia, Pennsylvania.

Bullinger, Ethelbert W. (1975). *A Critical Lexicon and Concordance to the English and Greek New Testament*. Regency Reference. Grand Rapids, Michigan.

Burgess, Harold, W. (1996). *Models of Religious Education*. Bridgepoint/Victor Books. Wheaton, Illinois.

Cates, Dr. Paul W. (1975). "A Christian Philosophy of Christian

Education." Association of Christian Schools. Hialeah, Florida (www.faithchristianmin.org/articles/cpe.htm).

CLASS Homeschools (2002). "Worldview – Philosophy of Education." Christian Liberty Academy School System, Christian Liberty Press. Arlington Heights, Illinois (www.homeschools. org/worldview/philosophyOfChristianEducation.html).

Colquhoun, Frank. (1984). *Four Portraits of Jesus: Christ in the Gospels*. InterVarsity Press. Downers Grove, Illinois.

Donne, John (2001). *The Complete Poetry and selected Prose of John Donne*. The Modern Library Press. New York, New York.

Edersheim, Alfred (1994). *Sketches of Jewish Social Life*. Hendrickson Publishers, Inc. Peabody, Massachusetts.

Eliot, T. S. (1967). *Christianity and Culture*. Harcourt, Inc. San Diego, California.

Evans, William (1974). *The Great Doctrines of the Bible*. Moody Press. Chicago, Illinois.

Gaebelein, Frank (1968). *Patterns of God's Truth*. Moody Press. Chicago, Illinois.

Gangel, Kenneth O., and Howard G. Hendricks (1988). *The Christian Educator's Handbook on Teaching*. Victor Books. United States.

Gardner, John (1977). *The Life and Times of Chaucer*. Vintage Books. New York, New York.

Garner, Carl B. (2003). *Jesus, The Master Teacher*. SWSBS.edu Publications. www.swsbs.edu/pages/writings/Garner.

Geisler, Dr. Norman (2002). *Systematic Theology: Volume 1*. Bethany House, Minneapolis, Minnesota.

Halley, Henry H. (1962). *Halley's Bible Handbook*. Zondervan Publishing House. Grand Rapids, Michigan.

Henry, Carl F. H. (1982). *God, Revelation, and Authority Volume V: God Who Stands and Stays, Part 1*. Crossway Books. Wheaton, Illinois.

Henry, Matthew. (1990). *Matthew Henry's Commentary on the Whole Bible: Volume 5*. World Bible Publishers. Iowa Falls, Iowa.

Hicks, David V. (1999). *Norms and Nobility*. University Press of America, Inc. Lanham, Maryland. Cumnor Hill, Oxford.

Hines, William L. (1997). *Leaving Yesterday Behind: A Victim No More*. Great Britain: Christian Focus Publications.

Hodge, Charles. (2003). *Systematic Theology*. Hendrickson Publishers.

Holmes, Arthur F. (1975). *The Idea of a Christian College*. Revised Edition. William B. Eerdmans Publishing Company. Grand Rapids, Michigan.

Horne, Herman Harrell (1998). *Jesus the Teacher*. Kregel Publications. Grand Rapids, Michigan.

Horne, Herman Harrell (1920). *The Teaching Techniques of Jesus*. Kregel Publications. Grand Rapids, Michigan.

Jaeger, Werner (1944). *Paideia, The Ideals of Greek Culture: Volume III*. Oxford University Press. Oxford. New York.

Jaeger, Werner (1961). *Early Christianity and Greek Paideia*. The Belknap Press of Harvard University Press. Cambridge, Massachusetts. London, England.

Jensen, Irving L. (1981). *Jensen's Survey of the New Testament*. Moody Press. Chicago, Illinois.

Keener, Craig S. (1993). *The IVP Bible Background Commentary*. InterVarsity Press. Downers Grove, Illinois.

Lioy, Dan. (2003). *Doctrine of the Holy Spirit Classroom Notes*. Independently published. Trinity Seminary. Newburg, Indiana.

Montgomery, John Warwick. (1995). *Faith Founded on Fact* (FF). Trinity College Publishing, Indiana.

Montgomery, John Warwick. (1995). *The Suicide of Christian Theology* (ST). Trinity College Publishing. Indiana.

Montgomery, John Warwick. (2002). *History, Law and Christianity*. Canadian Institute for Law, Theology, and Public Policy. Edmonton, AB, Canada.

Moreland, J. P., and William Lane Craig. (2003). *Philosophical Foundations for a Christian Worldview*. InterVarsity Press. Downers Grove, Illinois.

Morgan, G. Campbell. (1992). *The Gospel According to Luke*. Fleming H. Revell Press. Grand Rapids, Michigan.

Morris, Henry M. (1977). *Education for the Real World*. Creation-Life Publishers. San Diego, California.

Morris, Henry M. (1995). *The Defender's Study Bible*. World Bible Publishers. Iowa Falls, Iowa.

Nixon, Les. (2003). *Jesus: The Master Teacher*. Outback Patrol Publications (www.outbackpatrol.com.au/masterteacher.htm).

Packer, J. I., eds. Merrill C. Tenney and William White Jr. (1980). *The Bible Almanac*. Guidepost Publishing. Carmel, New York.

Pazmiño, Robert W. (1992). *Principles and Practices of Christian Education*. Wipf and Stock Publishers. Eugene, Oregon.

Pazmiño, Robert W. (1997). *Foundational Issues in Christian Education*. Baker Books. Grand Rapids, Michigan.

Riesen, Richard A. (2002). *Piety and Philosophy*. ACW Press. Phoenix, Arizona.

Robertson, A. T. (1930). *Word Pictures in the New Testament*. Broadman Press. Nashville, Tennessee.

Ryle, J. C. (1987). *Foundations of Faith*. Bridge Publishing, Inc. South Plainfield, New Jersey.

Schaeffer, Francis (1982). "Francis Schaeffer on Education: Priorities 1982." L'Abri, Switzerland (www.gbt.org/text/f.html).

Smith, Chuck. (1996). *Living Water: The Power of the Holy Spirit in Your Life*. Harvest House Publishers. Eugene, Oregon.

Sproul, R. C. (1989). *Ethics and the Christian.* Tyndale House Publishing. Wheaton, Illinois.

Trueblood, Elton (1965). *The Humor of Christ.* Harper & Row Publishers. New York, New York.

Tye, Karen (2000). *Basics of Christian Education.* Chalice Press. St. Louis, Missouri.

Walvoord, John F. (1991). *The Holy Spirit.* Zondervan Publishing House. Grand Rapids, Michigan.

Willard, Dallas (11/2003). "Jesus the Logician." (www.dwillard.org/ articles/printable.asp?artid=39).

Wilson, Douglas (1991). *Recovering the Lost Tools of Learning.* Crossway Books. Wheaton, Illinois.

Wilson, Douglas (2003). *The Case for Classical Christian Education.* Crossway Books. Wheaton, Illinois.

Yount, Rick (2000). "Jesus, the Master Teacher. The Teaching Ministry of the Church" (www.ministryserver.com/bible/lectures).

Zodhiates, Spiros (1991). *The Hebrew-Greek Key Word Study Bible.* AMG Publishers. Chattanooga, Tennessee.

WORKS CONSULTED

Adler, Mortimer J., Peter Wolff (1959). *A General Introduction to the Great Books and to a Liberal Education*. Encyclopedia Britannica, Inc. Chicago, Illinois.

Allott, Stephen (1974). *Alcuin of York, ca. AD 732–804: His Life and Letters*. Williams Sessions Limited. York, England.

Barzun, Jacques (1945). *Teacher in America*. Liberty Press. Indianapolis, Indiana.

Berkhof, Louis, and Cornelius Van Til (1953). *Foundations of Christian Education: Addresses to Christian Teachers*. Presbyterian and Reformed Publishing Company. Phillipsburg, New Jersey.

Blamires, Harry (1988). *Recovering the Christian Mind: Meeting the Challenge of Secularism*. InterVarsity Press. Downers Grove, Illinois.

Bolt, John (1993). *The Christian Story and the Christian School*. Christian Schools International. Grand Rapids, Michigan.

Braley, James, Jack Layman, and Ray White / ACSI (2003). *Foundations of Christian School Education*. Association of Christian Schools International. Colorado Springs, Colorado.

Bresland, Ronald W. (1999). *The Backward Glance: C. S. Lewis and Ireland*. Institute of Irish Studies. Belfast, Ireland.

Byrne, H. W. (1961). *A Christian Approach to Education*. Zondervan Publishing House, Grand Rapids, Michigan.

Cairns, Earle E. (1996). *Christianity Through the Centuries*. Zondervan Publishing House. Grand Rapids, Michigan.

Clark, Gordon H. (1946). *A Christian Philosophy of Education*. The Trinity Foundation. Jefferson, Maryland.

Clark, Gordon H. (1968). *An Introduction to Christian Philosophy*. The Trinity Foundation. Jefferson, Maryland.

Clark, Gordon H., and Aurelius Augustine (1986 / 1938). *Lord God of Truth / Concerning the Teache*r. The Trinity Foundation. Hobbs, New Mexico.

Colson, Charles W. and Nancy Pearcey (1999). *How Now Shall We Live?* Tyndale House Publishers, Inc. Wheaton, Illinois.

Dabney, R. L. (1996). *On Secular Education*. Canon Press. Moscow, Idaho.

Downs, Perry G. (1994). *Teaching for Spiritual Growth*. Zondervan Publishing House. Grand Rapids, Michigan.

Eavey, Charles B. (1964). *History of Christian Education*. Moody Press. Chicago, Illinois.

Edlin, Richard J. (1999). *The Cause of Christian Education*. Association of Christian Schools International. Colorado Springs, Colorado.

Gaebelein, Frank E. (1954). *The Pattern of God's Truth*. Moody Press. Chicago, Illinois.

Gaebelein, Frank E. (1985). *The Christian, the Arts, and Truth*. Multnomah Press. Portland, Oregon.

Gaebelein, Frank E. (1995). *Christian Education in a Democracy*. Association of Christian Schools International. Colorado Springs, Colorado.

Gardner, John (1977). *The Life and Times of Chaucer*. Vintage Books. New York, New York.

González, Justo L. (1984). *The Story of Christianity*. Prince Press. Peabody, Massachusetts.

Gregory, John Milton (1995). *The Seven Laws of Teaching*: Revised Edition. Baker Books. Grand Rapids, Michigan.

Hegeman, David Bruce (1999). *Plowing in Hope.* Canon Press. Moscow, Idaho.

Jensen, DeLamar (1992). *Reformation Europe.* D. C. Heath and Company. Lexington, Massachusetts.

Jensen, DeLamar (1992). *Renaissance Europe.* D. C. Heath and Company. Lexington, Massachusetts.

Jones, Douglas, and Douglas Wilson (1998). *Angels in the Architecture.* Canon Press. Moscow, Idaho.

Kienel, Paul A. (1998). *A History of Christian School Education.* Association of Christian Schools International. Colorado Springs, Colorado.

Kienel, Paul A., Ollie E. Gibbs, and Sharon R. Berry (1995). *Philosophy of Christian School Education.* Association of Christian Schools International. Colorado Springs, Colorado.

Knowles, Malcolm (1975). *Self-Directed Learning.* Cambridge Adult Education. Englewood Cliffs, New Jersey.

Latourette, Kenneth Scott (1953). *A History of Christianity*: Volume I: Beginnings to AD 1500. Harper San Francisco/HarperCollins Publisher. New York, New York.

LeBar, Lois E. (1958). *Education That is Christian.* Fleming H. Revell Company. Westwood, New Jersey.

Lewis, C. S. (1944). *The Abolition of Man.* Touchstone/Simon and Schuster. New York, New York.

Lewis, C. S. (1956). *Surprised by Joy.* Harcourt Brace Publishers. New York, New York.

Lloyd-Jones, D. Martyn (1989). *The Life of Joy and Peace.* Baker Books. Grand Rapids, Michigan.

Lockerbie, D. Bruce (1994). *A Passion for Learning.* Moody Press. Chicago, Illinois.

Macaulay, Susan Schaeffer (1984). *For the Children's Sake.* Crossway Books. Wheaton, Illinois.

Machen, J. Gresham (1987). *Education, Christianity and the State.* The Trinity Foundation. Hobbs, New Mexico.

McGrath, Alister (2001). *In the Beginning.* Doubleday. New York, New York.

Lightfoot, J. B., eds. Alister McGrath and J. I. Packer (1994). *Philippians.* Crossway Books. Wheaton, Illinois. Nottingham, England.

Montgomery, John Warwick (1969). *Where is History Going?* Bethany House Publishers. Minneapolis, Minnesota.

Montgomery, John Warwick (1975). *The Shape of the Past.* Bethany Fellowship, Inc. Minneapolis, Minnesota.

Montgomery, John Warwick (2002). *History, Law and Christianity.* Canadian Institute for Law, Theology and Public Policy. Edmonton, AB, Canada.

Moreland, J. P. (1997). *Love Your God With All Your Mind.* NavPress. Colorado Springs, Colorado.

Nixon, Brian C. (2003). *Inspired to Teach.* Calvary Chapel Publishing. Santa Ana, California.

Perks, Stephen C. (1992). *The Christian Philosophy of Education Explained.* Avant Books. North Yorkshire, England.

Peterson, Michael L. (1986). *Philosophy of Education.* InterVarsity Press. Downers Grove, Illinois.

Richards, Lawrence O., Gary J. Bredfeldt, and Larry Richards (1998). *Creative Bible Teaching.* Moody Press. Chicago, Illinois.

Schaeffer, Francis A. (1968). *Escape from Reason.* InterVarsity Press. Downers Grove, Illinois.

Schaeffer, Francis A. (1972). *He is There and He is Not Silent.* Tyndale House Publishers. Wheaton, Illinois.

Schindler, Claude E. Jr., and Pacheco Pyle (1997). *Still Educating for Eternity.* Association of Christian Schools International. Colorado Springs, Colorado.

Schuller, David S. (1993). *Rethinking Christian Education*. Chalice Press. St. Louis, Missouri.

Shelley, Bruce L. (1982). *Church History in Plain Language*. Word Publishing. Dallas, Texas.

Stern, David. (1998). *Complete Jewish Bible*. Jewish New Testament Publications, INC. Clarksville, Maryland.

Stott, John R. W. (1972). *Your Mind Matters*. InterVarsity Press. Downers Grove, Illinois.

Veith, Gene Edward Jr., and Andrew Kern (2001). *Classical Education: Towards the Revival of American Schooling*. Capital Research Center. Washington, DC.

Vos, J. G. (no date given). *What is Christian Education?* Reformed Presbyterian Church of N.A. Board of Education. Pittsburgh, Pennsylvania.

Wilhoit, James C., and John M. Dettoni (1995). *Nurture That is Christian*. Baker Books. Grand Rapids, Michigan.

Willard, Dallas (1997). *The Divine Conspiracy*. Harper San Francisco/HarperCollins Publishers. New York, New York.

Willard, Dallas (2002). *Renovation of the Heart*. Navpress. Colorado Springs, Colorado.

Wilson, Douglas (1999). *The Paideia of God*. Canon Press. Moscow, Idaho.

Wilson, Douglas (2001). *Excused Absence*. CruXpress. Mission Viejo, California.

Wise, Jessie, and Susan Wise Bauer (1999). *The Well-Trained Mind*. W. W. Norton & Company. New York, New York.

ABOUT THE AUTHOR

Brian C. Nixon is superintendent of schools at Calvary Chapel of Costa Mesa, California. He is a frequent lecturer on the subjects of education and church history. Besides his love for teaching, Brian enjoys music and spending time with his family.